*Blue Skies*

# Blue Skies

*Beyond The Dark Clouds Of Broken Thinking*

Paula Masters

# Table of Contents

# *Introduction*

⟶

I F YOU COULD TRAVEL ANYWHERE in the world, where would you most like to go? There are endless possibilities, and each one is aesthetically beautiful in its own way. But what if I told you that it is possible for the mind to journey to the most glorious destination of all? Not a physical location such as Mexico or Switzerland, but a spiritual one where health and strength can be found. This is what *Blue Skies* is all about. For those of us whose minds are wearied and broken from the storms of life, it is the most desirous of places—one to which earthly travel does not compare.

Even as Christians, we may have spent most of our lives stuck behind the dark clouds that accompany broken thinking. Insecurity, neediness, inadequacy, bitterness, discouragement, depression, and hopelessness bog us down. These emotions mixed with the expectations that come with the Christian culture can be a recipe for failure. When biblical precepts are pursued with no true connection to the meaning and power behind them, we are left in the same place we were before—broken.

In this book, you won't find any clichés or religious prescriptions to make you a cookie-cutter thinker. There will be no pat answers or bandages to cover your wounds. Guilt and pressure will have no part in our venture. What you will find here is an invitation to travel beyond the dark clouds of broken thinking to the blue skies above and beyond. Each chapter opens with interesting destinations, but they are simply reflections of a greater journey, a pilgrimage for our minds that awakens our spiritual senses as we scale unprecedented heights. Journeying past formulas and anecdotes into the realm of sacred intimacy with God, we find our souls moved in a way that brings divine healing for our wearied minds.

# CHAPTER 1

## Think about These Things
## Part One

~⌒~

I MAGINE STANDING ON THE SHORELINE of a sandy white beach where sunbeams shimmer like crystals on the water's surface. You are here in search of relief from life's wearisome struggles. Taking a deep breath, you let out a long, wistful sigh. You're certain the sights and sounds of the ocean will soothe your heavy mind. A wave gently splashes over your toes, covering your feet with a layer of soft sand. As quickly as the wave comes in, it recedes, and the powdery grains are washed out to sea. You can't help but wonder what it would be like if the waters could carry off your burdens and anxieties in the same way.

Surely, there must be someplace where you can find relief. Your thoughts drift to the story of the healing pool of Bethesda in the book of John, chapter 5. You think about what the anticipation at that basin must have felt like. Maybe a little like your thoughts at the shoreline but with much greater angst, of course. You realize there was something uniquely divine about the pool that stirred one's heart deep with hope. To step in it meant sure deliverance from crippling infirmities. Contact with the water meant the prison doors of sickness would swing open in an instant, and you would be free. Can you imagine the one poor soul who dreamed of being immersed in its fullness but could never quite reach it? Maybe that's how you feel right now. You have the same impression about your life. You want to do a better job at handling your emotions, but you continually fall short. You are perplexed as to why you make the same mistakes over and over again. Discouragement sets in, and relief feels so far away. Trying to make sense of it, you wonder if the problem is life—or perhaps you.

Does this sound familiar? We all feel like this on some level; it is the human condition. We are flawed individuals living in a fallen world. The good news is that within the chaos of life's brokenness lies a sacred journey meant for the believing heart, one that travels safely through the darkened clouds of self-defeating thought patterns into the blue skies intended for the redeemed mind.

The first order of business, however, is to convince yourself that there may actually be a good reason you are wearied

Consider this riddle: Three frogs were sitting on a log, floating in a pond. One decided to jump into the water. How many frogs were left on the log? I have opened a few workshops with this question, and it has generated some interesting dialogue. Naturally, when a riddle is posed, people try not to give the obvious response, which in this case would be two. And of course, since the subject at hand is the influence of our thinking, one might be inclined to give an answer that suggests that the two other frogs were persuaded to take the plunge, thus making the answer zero. But here's the twist on this particular brainteaser: the frog in question decided to jump but never followed through. Consequently, all three frogs are still sitting snugly on the log.

The point is this: what we think is often very different from what we do. This riddle shows the propensity to focus so intently on behavior that we neglect the mind. As Christians, we can get pretty caught up in how we appear. Depending on our backgrounds, we may even be carrying a weight of guilt of never quite measuring up to what has been expected of us in terms of performance. Interestingly, it's often the religious community that makes superficial presentation synonymous with successful Christian living.

Yet, this has never been God's intention. In fact, let me offer this encouragement. If you recognize that you don't have it all together, you are actually farther along than those who feel confident in their own abilities. Why?

Because those who admit their *inability* are the ones able to recognize their need of God's grace.

Grace—our full acceptance in Christ, through Christ—is all we need.

Something my husband told me before we got married really underscores this truth perfectly. I was hesitant to make a commitment because I had come from a difficult background and had a tendency to operate out of fear. I felt bad for my husband, who was dating me at the time. So, I let him know this was something I needed to change before we moved forward in our relationship.

What he said next astounded me.

"Paula, if you are able to change, life will be easier for you, but if you never change, I will still marry you, and I'll always desire to be married to you for the rest of my life."

Wow! Those words gave me the courage I needed to move forward. In his willingness to absorb my past, present, and future brokenness, I was liberated. Those grace-filled words gave me just the impetus I needed to change inwardly.

So it is with Christ. Of course He would love to see us relinquish our broken thinking, but He wants this for our sakes, not His. On top of this, He loves us perfectly and wholly whether we change or not. He has already absorbed our sins—every one we have ever committed or will commit. Finally, we can breathe easier. Performance only appears impressive, but in reality, it is futile. Ephesians 4:17 reminds us that we don't have to live this way anymore: "you should no longer walk…in the futility of your mind." The word *futility* can be translated as "vanity"—trying to look as if we have it all together. It's vain, empty thinking, and God has so much more for our minds.

Feeling the freedom to fail is essential to the health of our minds. We can rest secure in the knowledge that God is concerned with the redemption of our thinking through grace because He loves us and cares about our spiritual well-being—not because He wants trophies. When we realize this is the intent of His heart, it inspires us to make changes that will benefit us spiritually and emotionally. God is genuinely interested in our inward healing, and it often takes going through many failures to get there.

## The role of the mind

Now we can shift our focus from behavior to what's going on in the mind. Isaiah 26:3–4 confirms the significance of the mind's role—even revealing it to be the key that unlocks our hearts to a pilgrimage of peace.

Notice the emphasis:

> You will keep in perfect peace whose mind is stayed on you, because he trusts in you. (Isaiah 26:3–4)

It does not say those who serve and obey Him, but rather those whose minds are engaged and set on Him and who journey with Him through the thick and thin of life.

For our time together in this book, we will do just that as we set our sights on a passage of scripture that will drive this reality into the deepest parts our hearts. Take a moment to pause between each phrase as you read the following verse:

> Finally, brothers and sisters, whatever is true, whatever is honorable, whatever is just, whatever is pure, whatever is lovely, whatever is commendable, if there is anything worthy of praise, think about these things. (Philippians 4:8)

On the surface, these words may strike us as nothing more than pleasant sentiments, but there is rich substance to be uncovered here. In fact, sometimes it takes a second touch to our spiritual sight to help us see the hidden view meant only for the gaze of the soul.

Here's what I mean. Many Christians don't realize there are two levels of divine understanding. The first is a general view. For instance, a person might be correct in their evaluation that this passage is lovely and noble, yet they might lack clarity of vision into its deeper meaning. This general view is a learned view and is a dim picture of God's intended purpose for our thoughts.

The second level of understanding is an experiential view that changes our spiritual vision from dim to clear—it is God's glory unveiled inwardly. This redemptive and powerful vision can be had only through the transforming salve of the Spirit applied to the eyes of our minds. It is the second touch of sight where spiritual things no longer look cloudy or seem ill defined.

This book is a purposeful exploration into this exceptional dimension.

> And he took the blind man by the hand and led him out of the village, and when he had spit on his eyes and laid his hands on him, he asked him, "Do you see anything?" And he looked up and said, "I see men, but they look like trees, walking." Then Jesus laid his hands on his eyes again; and he opened his eyes, his sight was restored, and he saw everything clearly. (Mark 8:23–25)

Metaphorically speaking, we may have been staring at dark clouds for so long that we are unable to perceive the majestic blue skies beyond them. A vast and beautiful heavenly realm awaits our attention.

## The weight that lifts us up

We start with the phrase "think about these things" (Philippians 4:8). The word *think* in the original Greek language of the New Testament has the meaning of "reckoning, calculating, or weighing." This implies that a divine weight of truth is embedded or even hidden in this passage, intended for our minds to comprehend. To think about these things means that we must search out this divine weight. No longer settling for superficial facts, we ponder its deeper meaning and allow it to change our world.

To reckon is not to imagine this weight into being but to think on that which already is. In other words, a spiritual weight exists, and it is ours to discover.

Let's look at the mention of volume (weight) elsewhere in scripture:

According to the riches of his glory may he grant you to be strengthened with power through his Spirit in your inner being, so that
Christ may dwell in your heart by faith—that you, being rooted
and grounded in love, may have strength to comprehend with all the
saints what is the breadth and length and height and depth, and to
know the love of Christ, that surpasses knowledge, that you may be
filled with all the fullness of God. (Ephesians 3:16–19)

Notice the spiritual substance mentioned in these verses is described in terms
of dimension, as having breadth, length, height, and depth. If that weren't
enough to confirm that spiritual poundage exists, the passage ends with Paul's
hope that we be filled with the complete fullness of this weight (which is
God).

This comes as no surprise because the Bible talks about God's glory in
terms of weight. In fact, the Hebrew word for glory is *kabod*, which literally
means "weight." As Jonathan Edwards put it, "The glory of God is the weight
of all God is." What we begin to grasp as God opens our minds is the amazing
reality of spiritual weight.

With fresh insight into the meaning of the word *think*, we can rightly
ascertain that we are being directed to calculate the spiritual dimension found
in Philippians 4:8. In fact, each chapter of this book unveils the mind-bog-
gling reality that God's truth is revealed to our thinking in the form of divine
weight.

But before we discover that, let's examine how our minds function because
the mind is the instrument God designed to do all our thinking, calculating,
and reckoning. Envision the mind as a sponge. When you dip a sponge into a
bucket of water, the sponge soaks up the water, and when you pull the sponge
out, it is heavier than it was when it was dry. Our minds are similar; they
soak in the waters that they are exposed to in life both good and bad. This
includes all that we are exposed to of a nonspiritual nature. In other words,
our entire lifetime will be a matter of either soaking in spiritual or nonspiritual substance.

Colossians 3:2 draws the distinction between these two weights in clear terms. "Set your mind on the things above, not on earthly things." As we evaluate the effects of these two opposing weights, we begin to understand why we struggle when difficulties come our way. This makes sense because earthly weight—anxiety, worry, thoughts of discouragement—can weigh down the mind, making it difficult to find the fullness of peace that it longs for.

We must note that scripture is not implying that we should disengage in earthly activities. After all, God designed us to live on Earth. The instruction *not to set our minds on earthly things* is talking about the worldly agenda that excludes Christ's heavenly purposes.

Peter is a good example. Interestingly, Peter's intention seemed reasonable and compassionate. Here's how it went down: Jesus, sharing with His disciples that He must suffer, explained that He would be killed and raised back to life on the third day. Peter, being concerned for Christ's well-being, pulled Jesus aside and told Him he was not going to let this happen. Scripture even uses the word *rebuke*, as if to indicate that Peter was scolding Jesus for sounding so bleak and hopeless. What Peter didn't recognize was that this very path he was trying to prevent Jesus from taking would bring salvation to the world.

Jesus's reply to Peter—"Get behind Me, Satan"—is startling, yet it reveals the core of the problem. As thoughtful as this gesture seemed, Peter's motivation was based on an earthly priority that excluded Christ's heavenly purposes. It went against the Father's will for His Son—that He would be the sacrifice for our sins. This in turn lined up with Satan's objective to interfere with God's higher design. In Jesus's poignant admonition, there was a redirection of weight. The spiritual needed to take precedence over the nonspiritual and temporal.

What made Peter go down this line of thinking in the first place? The answer becomes clear in Jesus's response: "You are not mindful of the things of God, but of the things of men." Amazingly, the crux of all brokenness can be discovered in the one small but revealing word: *mindful.* You see, what our minds are full of makes a difference—not to our salvation, but in the ways we are affected by the things that have a hold on our minds. What our minds are full of will automatically have a weight of influence in our lives.

Each one of us carries the weight of whatever our thinking is soaked with. Even in this instant, something is influencing our thought-life. Consider the common struggle of insecurity. Insecurity is an anxiety-provoking emotion that causes us to feel nervous, uncomfortable, and unsure of ourselves. As a result, we do everything from avoiding social situations to overcompensating in an effort to cope with the unbearable heaviness of this constricting emotion. In one simple moment, our thoughts can transport us to a cold, dark place of uncertainty and instability—and it is all a product of what our minds are full of at the time.

Yet, if we could peer beyond its cumbersome presence, we would recognize that insecurity speaks of the need to place our confidence in something greater than ourselves, something of superior weight. The spiritual journey that is meant for the mind lifts us to a sacred place where new thinking can flourish. From God's vantage point, a peaceful, serene sanctuary lies just beyond the ominous, dark clouds. This sanctuary is not seen in formulas, behavioral modifications, or clichés so obviously placed in plain view. It is hidden at a deeper level that is discovered only by the seeking heart.

So our journey begins, dipping our toes ever so slightly into healing waters.

*Questions to Ponder:*

1. To reckon and calculate doesn't mean to imagine something into being but to think on that which already exists. Our focus phrase, "Think on these things," is asking us to reckon and calculate spiritual weight. Can you describe a past spiritual experience during which you felt the heavy weight of its impact in your life? How did that affect your heart and subsequent behavior?

2. The mind is like a sponge that soaks in the weight of whatever our thoughts are full of. Can you identify a weight that your mind has been full of in the past week? How did that affect your behavior?

3. Insecurity is an example of a weighty emotion that can flood the mind. Identify an emotion that plays a heavy role in your thinking.

# Think about These Things
## Part Two

⤙

C AN YOU IMAGINE A TIME when going to Mars might be a common option for the adventurous traveler? Before venturing beyond Earth's atmosphere, astronauts are taught the dynamics of weightlessness, the opposite of what is natural to us as humans. They are put into simulators to experience what it feels like. This is because understanding the effects of gravity is critical to maneuvering space travel successfully.

The same is true for us as we determine the effect that heaviness has on our minds and ultimately our daily life. For us to successfully navigate through dark clouds of broken thinking, we must gain a better understanding of the concept of weight.

Considering the state of our minds at the point of birth (natural and spiritual) will help us see the weighty complexity of broken thinking and understand why it happens. Notice the contrast in the following analogy of the mind at the time of new life.

An infant is born pure and without defilement. Of course I am speaking figuratively because we are all born into this world unregenerate, but an infant has no conscious awareness of sin. When the infant first arrives on the scene of life, she is weightless in terms of exposure. As the infant grows into the toddler years, she soaks in layers of life's exposures to the mind. This can be anything: environment, tragedies, mistreatment, boundary issues, abuse, sin, and any number of negative experiences. Over the years, these layers of weight build up, soaking deep into the pores of her mind, causing it to gradually become more and more broken and more like the negative influences that did the breaking.

Now consider this. When a Christian is born into the family of God, the complete opposite happens. At the point of salvation, the mind is already broken from the layers of weight absorbed over the years. The process that begins at the moment of salvation is a gradual undoing of these layers. The heart has been redeemed and clothed in God's righteousness, but the mind and many years of wrong thinking are still in need of rescue. Each phrase in our focus passage is divinely designed to do just that—to set us free, layer by layer.

In this section, we will examine some of the weights of broken thinking that we carry throughout our lives until we are raised above them by the power of God's grace.

## Weights from the past

But first, let me share with you a story to give you an example of how this looks in the real world. A couple wanted to adopt a little girl. They had been praying for years that God would bring just the right child into their family. They finally received a call that a ten-year-old girl was available for adoption. This little girl was born into a good and loving home. Both of her parents had been killed instantly in an automobile accident, and there were no remaining relatives. Oddly, within the very same week, the adoptive couple received another call about a different girl available for adoption, also ten years old. This girl's circumstances were very different. Her parents were alive but had been extremely abusive. They told her she was too filthy to sleep in her bed, so every night this little girl took her ragged little blanket and slept on the floor at the foot of the bed. Of course this news saddened the prospective adoptive parents. Although they had planned on adopting only one little girl, they prayed and decided to adopt both.

When they brought the girls home, one of the first things the new parents did was to sit them both down and explain to them they were dedicated to loving them, nurturing them, and providing for them equally with no favoritism. At bedtime, they brought the girls upstairs to a beautiful bedroom with two brightly decorated beds, one for each girl. After the girls chose which bed they wanted, they said their good nights. A few minutes later, the parents went back to the room to check on the girls. Peeking through the doorway, they were surprised to find that the little girl who had come from an abusive background was not in her bed. As they scanned the room, they quickly spotted her on the floor, sound asleep at the foot of the bed. Why do you suppose she was there? Years of weight in her mind were still present, even though her life had completely changed for the better and she was now in a loving, safe home.

It is the same with us. When we become Christians, we are brought into the family of God, but we each bring very different life experiences to this new role. Our ability to adapt in our new position as adopted children in this heavenly kinship often depends on the weights we have struggled to carry throughout our lives. This happens even when we know without a doubt that we have been forgiven and have as much access to God's love as anyone else has. This is because the weightiness of broken thinking can keep us bogged down and unable to receive love and forgiveness or to move forward in all that is available to us in terms of spiritual growth, much like the little girl in this story. The weight of grace has rescued our souls but has not yet permeated our minds with its fullness. It takes time for God's grace to become divinely personal to us.

## Weights from the world

The story of the adopted girls is a great example of the power that the wrong kind of weight can have on the mind, as well as its ongoing influence—even if we have been Christians for many years. It is similar to being impaired by or under the influence. Here's what I mean. 1 John 5:19 states that the whole world lies under the sway of the wicked one. The word *sway* means "being under the influence." In the same way that drugs and alcohol dull our physical senses, the weight of wrong thinking dulls our senses to spiritual growth and understanding. This means that just because we read the word of God doesn't mean we hear its eternal truths in the depths of our hearts because our spiritual hearing is dulled. We can't understand God's word because earthly burdens are impairing our spiritual sight. We feel weak and unable to move forward in life as we watch others pass us by—as in the story of the man at the pool of Bethesda. Our thoughts naturally affect our behavior, like the little girl in our story. She was still under the influence of the massive weights from her past.

So here we sit with our insecurities, inferiorities, and other identity issues, even though we are told that God completely loves and accepts us. We say we believe this, but it has not fully penetrated because the pores of our minds are still saturated with the weight of broken thinking that has formed over the years. This is especially prevalent in the church. We are often brought up to believe that our behavior is what God really cares about, but this only proves that we really don't believe He loves and accepts us without reservation. The weight of wrong thinking has obstructed the fullness of this truth to the core of our being. We need redemption in our thinking.

Does the Bible mention the consequences being filled with weight? 1 Corinthians 3:1–4 touches on the inability to receive solid food because of being filled with nonspiritual thoughts. Paul goes so far as to say he could not address the Christians in Corinth as spiritual people but only as carnal.

The Greek word for *carnal* means "fleshly," but carnality of the mind is often harder to pinpoint and goes deeper than obvious sin. You can see proof of this in our belief systems in the traditional church. For instance, we may never consider being morally legalistic as carnal—yet it is. Jesus spoke out against this very sin that lurked in the hearts of the scribes and Pharisees. Why? Because it dwells in the fleshly mind.

The weight of legalism holds our minds captive in bondage, whereas the weight of grace has the power to lift us beyond rigid expectations of performance. If we allow the opposing weights of legalism and grace to coexist in our minds, we restrict our ability to live freely and confidently as daughters and sons of God. We continue to dip our minds in all sorts of pools where broken thinking flourishes.

In the following sections, we will take a closer look at various spiritual weights that we may not have realized are dwelling in our hearts and minds. I am not suggesting these are all bad. I am simply providing a springboard from which you can search your own heart for weights that might be keeping your mind from the fullness of spiritual health.

## The weight of conditioned thinking

This is where we have been conditioned to think in certain ways. For instance, if we were belittled over the years, we may have been conditioned to think that we are insignificant. But if we were encouraged to think too highly of ourselves, we may have been conditioned to be prideful. Or, if we have been brought up to think that everything must be organized at all times, we might have an inability to be spontaneous. On the other hand, if we were taught to be free spirited, we may have been conditioned with the inability to be structured. Conditioning is a type of influence that happens over time and through much repetition. In the church, we have often been conditioned to believe that we must exercise good behavior if we want to gain God's favor. The truth is that God looks only at our faith in Christ and what He has done on our behalf.

## The weight of worldly thinking

Worldly thinking is when we are influenced by the external structure of our individual world. This expands beyond the family into social groups, peers, trends, work, church, school, and organizations we are involved with. The hierarchical structure of our office environment and how it influences us may be different from the makeup of our family and the influence we receive there. At work, we may be devalued, but at home, we are highly valued, or vice versa. Difficult social structures are one of the reasons there is such a high rate of suicide among teenagers. If they are in a setting that tolerates bullying, teens often feel as if they cannot bear up under the weight. The influence we receive from these various settings can follow us for the rest of our lives.

The same applies to the political structure of our Christianity. If we have been under the theology of fire and brimstone, we may be influenced to have anxious feelings toward God. We may fear that He is angry with us, when the truth is that His anger passes over us because of the blood of Christ.

## The weight of influenced thinking

This is when prominent people in our lives influence our thinking. Sometimes, this is someone we admire greatly; other times, it is an overbearing individual, possibly someone we are intimidated by or feel compelled to impress. Perhaps we don't want to let this person down. Or we try to break free from his or her influence, only to find resistance. If our spiritual mentor has been critical or demanding, we may be influenced to think we can never measure up, when the truth is that when God looks at us, He sees us robed in Christ's righteousness.

## The weight of dispositional and personality thinking

Dispositional thinking is intrinsic to our individual nature. Maybe we are cynical, or perhaps we're too trusting. Some of us are thick skinned, whereas others are sensitive. We might be spirited, or we could be laid back. There is no end to the variations in personalities and dispositions. The type of person we are by virtue of our DNA and early childhood environment will have an influence on our thinking. If I am suspicious, I might be more inclined to jump to conclusions; if I am naive, I might be too willing to believe wrong things. Often our dispositions and personalities can shape faulty thoughts of God. If I am philosophical, I might be inclined to overintellectualize God. If I have more of an emotional bent, I might tend to overemotionalize my faith.

## The weight of idealistic thinking

Idealistic thinking is when we are driven by our own particular ideals. When they are not reached, our spirits are crushed. I had a seventeen-year-old girl in one of my workshops tell me this type of thinking really hit home with her when her parents' marriage began to fall apart. She felt traumatized that her ideals of the perfect marriage and family had been betrayed. When it comes to our Christian walk, maybe we haven't met our own idealistic expectations, so we withdraw from God and avoid fellowship with other Christians.

## The weight of uninformed thinking

Faulty thinking is when we form opinions without full information. This type of thinking is very common and hard to recognize because it is so automated. It is human nature to go along with what the majority thinks. In the church, we often absorb information without question, but the variety of denominations and religious perspectives in the world proves how confusing faith can be—so we end up following stylistic preference.

## The weight of cultural or environmental thinking

Cultural thinking is similar to conditioned thinking but is generally attached to strong cultural practices that have shaped our thoughts. For example, when we were children, if we were told to eat everything on our plate, we might still be compelled to do so, and not doing so causes guilt. This can also be termed *cultural conditioning*. We are all a product of our culture to some degree, whether we grew up on the streets or in a quiet, tree-lined suburb. Our religious backgrounds can have a very strong hold on our thinking, and the same is true for our ethnic backgrounds. We can see this in women who have grown up wearing head coverings. Even in liberal cultures, the ingrained influence causes them to continue wearing head scarves anyway. If we have been brought up in a Christian culture with certain rituals, such as conservative hymns, we may feel uneasy in a different church setting, such as a contemporary service with loud music, exuberant singing, hand clapping, and shouting.

## The weight of secret thinking

These are the secret thoughts that we would never share with anyone else, but just because no one sees our thoughts doesn't mean they don't have an influence on our thinking. If you have secretly wondered how God can really love you, there is great news in store for you in this book.

These are only a few examples of the weights of thinking that can have an effect on our lives—sometimes negative and sometimes positive. Reading these may have prompted an awareness in you that has now caused internal struggle. If you feel uncomfortable, that is a good sign, because identifying troublesome weights in our thinking is part of the process of breaking loose from the power of their control. When our minds marinate in negative influences for years, we naturally become influenced or impaired by them. Now we can see why we might have a harder time in a season of challenge than we hoped. Even if a plate of truth and grace were set before us, we might have some old patterns of thinking that keep us from feeding the deepest part of our minds with the nourishment that sets us free.

These kinds of weights (and many others) come with the inescapable challenges we face in life. But we need not dismay, because Philippians 4:8 unfolds a far greater weight from above. Even in suffering we can boldly proclaim we have superior hope. A refreshing rescue comes with spiritual weight.

Think about this. Wouldn't it be incredible if we could have our minds so saturated with truth that no matter our past, present, or future, our minds would be free? What a wonderful feeling that would be for any of us struggling with the crippling weight of broken thinking—like wading in the pool of Bethesda. Our identity in Christ would emerge as our old insecurities were washed away. Let me tell you, God has this in store for you, and more!

In closing this chapter, let me pose a question. In the story of the man at the pool of Bethesda, what gave him the ability to finally make it to the water? Perhaps he just needed some inspiration to get up and walk. After all, that is what Jesus told him to do. But we would be remiss if we ignored the life-changing point of this story. Remember, the man was incapable of making it to the edge of the pool. Notice also that Christ's instructions did not require the man to go into the pool. Why? Because this blessed invalid had come into contact with the Living Water—Jesus himself! There was no need for the pool of healing water once grace had met him in the form of Jesus.

The same is true for us. When we come to terms with the great weight of our inability, our personal contact with the weight of Christ's unlimited ability becomes our rescue. We can stop trying to be free through positive thinking and self-help techniques, and those don't last anyway. Deep inner healing requires the heavy-duty spiritual muscle of grace—robed in truth and delivered in love. It's time to let God throw His weight around in our minds. That is what this book is all about. Let's move forward into the unparalleled dimensions of weight found in Philippians 4:8. Blue skies await!

*Questions to Ponder:*

1. Can you relate to the adopted girl in our story who was under the influence of past thinking, even though her circumstances had changed? Are you under the influence of old thinking in a specific area of your life?
2. What might be an opposing spiritual weight to offset the weight of broken thinking in your life?
3. Of the eight examples of broken thinking, which one resonated with your life, and why?

CHAPTER 2

# *Whatever Is True*
# *Part One*

〜

I MAGINE TRAVELING TO THE MOST pristine destination you can
think of, a place that inspires serenity and peace. Perhaps Ireland
comes to mind with its emerald hills and lush rolling slopes. But
let's take this thought further—imagine there is a secret path where each step
leads to a greater and deeper transformation of character, a tranquil course
led by a wise, noble guide who cares deeply for your soul. Does this sound
farfetched? Incredibly, it is not. Consider this passage in scripture, and notice
the striking similarity:

> The LORD is my Shepherd…He makes me lie down in green pas-
> tures. He leads me besides still waters. He restores my soul. He leads
> me in paths of righteousness. (Psalm 23:3, 4)

This is only one of many vivid images in the Bible that display the truth of
an unseen yet active kingdom that we are currently a part of as the sons and
daughters of God.

Because conscious awareness of such a spiritual reality is fleeting, our minds
tend to wander to fictional places like Narnia, or Middle Earth in the *Lord of
the Rings* trilogy. I always think of the Dr. Seuss book *Horton Hears a Who!*
when my mind ventures to an imaginary world. Do you remember the story?

Inside a single blossom lives a tiny community so small it is not visible to the human eye. In this story, an elephant named Horton discovers this uniquely hidden city. At first, he is unable to convince the rest of the world of its thriving reality—not because it isn't there, but because it is concealed from their physical senses. Then, evidence of this little place called Whoville begins to surface.

It is amusing to contemplate, but there are some common themes between Whoville and the unseen world that God speaks about in the Bible. For one thing, just because it's hidden doesn't mean it's not there.

This chapter opens with an invitation to consider such a place—not an actual destination such as Ireland or a fictional one like the imaginary tiny village of Whoville but a real living community. After all, those who belong to God are part of this uniquely hidden city, this invisible spiritual kingdom that is thriving and in full operation. It's thrilling to contemplate! Yet, if we are honest with ourselves, we have to admit that we rarely think about it in such present terms, and we may even have difficulty believing it is real.

A. W. Tozer offers valuable spiritual realignment. In his book *The Pursuit of God*, he describes this mysterious dimension as "that which has existence apart from any idea any mind may have of it, and would exist if there were no mind anywhere to entertain a thought of it. That which is real has being in itself. It does not depend upon the observer for its validity."

In other words, *whatever is true* is an indestructible, unmovable reality that is not dependent on whether anyone believes it.

Our journey takes an adventurous route as we mine for *whatever is true* in this heavenly realm. Stepping into this unseen dominion divinely activates a rescuing process that is meant for our minds. Those gray clouds that seem so pervasive in our pools of broken thinking can't help but make way for blue skies of new thought attached to this sacred province, and not just in theology but in the engagement of our spiritual senses.

We will talk about all five spiritual senses as we make our way through this book, but we begin by delving into the sense of sight, the ability to take in truth through the gaze of the soul. Understanding what gives clarity to this divine lens is key.

The blind man we discussed in chapter 1 could not see until Jesus gave his eyes the ability to take in light, and the same is true for our spiritual eyes. As light is necessary for physical sight, so spiritual light is necessary to perceive the sacred kingdom we are part of. It is no coincidence that scripture uses the word *light* interchangeably with the word *truth*. In keeping with the subject of weight discussed in the previous chapter, we begin to understand that the weight of light is synonymous with the weight of truth. The light of truth has the power to open our eyes.

Of course, this can only be a partial experience while we dwell in our temporal bodies, but as the children of God, we have the ability to tap into greater dimensions of this spiritual sight than we may realize.

There is so much the naked eye cannot see that the spiritual eye has access to that it would take an entire lifetime to discover—and even then it would fall short. Consider the story of Saint Augustine, who at the time of his death awoke for a brief moment to say, "I have seen the Lord. All I have written is but straw." He was able to share a glimpse of heaven before passing from this earthly realm that was so full of light that he considered his teachings substandard. Yet, while on Earth, he was given great deposits of this light that he taught and wrote about in depth. His enlightened writings opened many eyes in his day, and still do.

Imagine for a moment if the eyes of your heart were completely illuminated and you could see the fullness of the kingdom of God unhindered. All your broken thinking would mend in an instant. It's hard to fathom such clarity because you would be able to see value for what it truly is. You might be surprised to find that some of the things you grip so tightly are not as important as you thought. Wisdom would flow nonstop, even greater than Solomon's, and you would be able to recognize danger, as well as good and wise direction. How clearly we could navigate this life if our eyes were opened in this way. Amazingly, much of what keeps us from such insight is the opposing weight of darkness, which blocks and dulls our abilities to process truth.

But even in seasons of darkened and impaired spiritual vision, light flourishes all around us unceasingly. Doubt does not change God's ever-present kingdom. I will venture a step further in saying that whatever is true of this spiritual realm is very real, and darkness is simply an altered reality or the masking of it. In other words, spiritual reality is real and permanent, but all that we see with our physical eyes will eventually fade away.

Albert Einstein suggested there is no such thing as darkness, only the absence of light. He offered the philosophy that darkness is an illusion that casts a shadow over light. He may very well have been on to something greater than he realized. Consider this verse that speaks of God:

> Even the darkness will not be dark to you; the night will shine like the day, for darkness is as light to you. (Psalm 139:12)

Thinking in these terms, we might say darkness conceals truth from our minds and is felt as a weighty absence of light. Even as believers, we often draw our sight through the darkened lens of whatever is blocking light. As a result, we find ourselves visually limited by influences that have impaired us in this life.

Confusion and obscurity naturally come with living in a broken world, but it has always been God's plan that the eyes of our hearts perceive the eternal purposes we were designed for. He desires His light to illuminate in a way that heightens our awareness outside the darkness. When this happens, it changes how we perceive His kingdom and our place in it, even now.

Darkness, on the other hand, keeps us focused inward. Or, we could say, inward focus keeps us in the dark. This is a very narrow view that limits us to self-centered and temporary thinking.

A good way to picture this is to imagine we're sitting in a large room in complete darkness with headphones on that block out all sound. All we can think about is what we are feeling—fear, anxiety, or restlessness, perhaps. We could be deluged with many thoughts and emotions, but one thing for certain is they will center on us.

Now imagine the light is switched on, and when we look around the room, we see that it is filled with people interacting with great enthusiasm.

We eagerly seek to find out what's going on, who the people are, and what the purpose is for this room besides just us. Our focus has shifted simply because of the infusion of light and the awakening of our senses.

Darkness undoubtedly causes us to lose sight of our kingdom connection; as a result, we travel inward, deeper into our brokenness. The divine light switch that we have access to as the children of God reverses this process. This light illuminates the eternal workings of a spiritual realm that we are actively part of. It takes us outside of ourselves and fills us with great purpose and direction.

## Darkness can masquerade as light

We must be careful, however, in identifying true light. Consider this interesting oxymoron: darkness can appear as light. Scripture says that Satan masquerades as an angel of light (2 Corinthians 11:14). This phenomenon is important to grasp in our journey to spiritual sight. Satan's light is a kind of darkness that shines brightly, but it stands in opposition to the truth of God's word. Therefore, it is a false light, a mere shadow and mirage that covers true light.

Many situations and experiences in our lives will present us with this kind of deception, and it can be confusing. Rescuing ourselves without relying on God falls into this category. Temporary relief can come from exploring substitute light sources, but if it is not the true light of Christ, it will not last, and it will cause us to remain in the dark.

Quite often when Christians are wounded by the church, they sink into a season of darkness. An example of this is when church leaders impose dogmatic expectations or a facade of religiosity. This misrepresents Christ and actually pushes people away from the church. If we've been hurt by a religious leader, we must remember that our relationship to God is based on the light of truth, and the offenses of careless Christians can't alter truth, even if they cast a shadow. Truth always remains securely in place, just like the brilliant blue sky that is always part of Earth's atmosphere even when shrouded by dark clouds.

## Knowledge without the Spirit

Even the written word of God can keep us in darkness when we misinterpret it or misuse it. Notice how Jesus called out the Pharisees for doing this:

> You study the Scriptures diligently because you think that in them you have eternal life. These are the very Scriptures that testify about me. (John 5:39)

The Bible is a God-given instrument to guide us in matters of faith, but we make a big mistake when we impose flawed adherences to God's word based on faulty human interpretations. The Bible was never meant to be held up as a higher entity than the truth it conveys. Scripture becomes holy only as the Spirit reveals the truth of Jesus to our hearts. When the Spirit brings these words to life, the Bible is transformed from a material document into divine expressions meant for the soul. Our eyes are then opened, and our sense of spiritual sight is awakened—unlike the Pharisees, who, for all their intense study of scripture, were still blind.

The Bible affects us similarly as individuals. As we are moved by its revelation, we become one with it. It begins to frame how we see our lives here on Earth connected to this sacred realm. This influences our thought-life, which then influences our affections. Consider what Paul said in 2 Corinthians 3:2: "You yourselves are our letter, written on our hearts, known and read by everyone." We reflect the word in the same way we embrace it. If we appropriate it with a legalistic mentality, our lives will reflect this, and others will perceive us as harsh and legalistic.

However, if our eyes are opened by grace to see the majesty of the One of whom the word was written, we are changed within—and others will perceive us as full of grace and light, merciful and forgiving instead of harsh, judgmental, and legalistic. As we allow the Bible to be a source of light for us, we become a source of light for others. This is the design of the kingdom life that we are a part of.

## *Our spiritual sense of sight*

God certainly uses earthly institutions such as churches and ministries in our lives, but our connection to whatever is true reaches far beyond these temporal entities. Each of us has been equipped with the God-given ability to access the heavenly kingdom personally without having to go through another person as an intermediary. We may feel limited because of layers of darkness, but we can be assured that progressive illumination is part of God's plan. There is light awaiting the eyes of our hearts.

We can see this analogy in the story of Lazarus when he was raised from the dead. Most people notice only the obvious—that is, Lazarus was brought back to life. But observe how this newly risen soul came out of the tomb, staggering and constrained. His hands and feet were bound, and his face was covered. He was completely wrapped in grave clothes. He was alive, but his senses were hindered by the coverings that had bound him in death. For Lazarus to fully live in the newness that Jesus had raised him to, these wrappings had to be removed so he could see, feel, and hear the world around him. He had to come alive to the new reality he had been given.

This journey from death to life is meant for us as children of God—life outside the tomb of darkness we've been shrouded in for so long in our broken thoughts. Yet, once outside, even more light awaits. Those grave clothes must come off if we are to experience the kingdom in the way God intends us to, the way He created us to experience it. God wants us to feel His presence, hear His voice, taste His goodness, smell the fragrance of His loveliness, and see the beauty of His truth. There is healing in this. It's a pilgrimage of the most exquisite kind, enlivening the senses of the soul while restoring health to the mind. Moving forward, we will see a shift of weight from the temporal to the eternal as the reality of the kingdom of God becomes more vivid in our thinking.

*Questions to Ponder:*

1. Can you identify some shadows that are falling on your day? (Emotions, self-focus, wrong perspectives)

2. Can you remember a time when God shone His light on a particular encounter, conversation, or event in your life that made you look at something from a spiritual perspective?

3. Identify a false light in your past that shone so brightly that it deceived you. Where did it lead, and when did you recognize it as being misleading?

# Whatever Is True
## Part Two

THROUGHOUT MY CHILDHOOD, A SET of about twenty boxes from my grandparents sat unopened in our garage no matter where we lived. As we moved from house to house, the boxes moved with us, and again they sat unopened. I was never quite sure what was in those boxes, but I knew they held family history. At the death of my paternal grandmother, they were sent to my father. It was obvious that the contents would shed light on our family connections, but they remained sealed as we went about our busy lives. Even after the passing of my parents, I brought the boxes to my garage, where for years they held a similar existence.

Then one day, I decided to open those mysterious boxes. I discovered all sorts of interesting family affiliations. There were photos, letters, and every kind of document you can imagine. Some of the items, such as a personal scrapbook, made me feel as if I were acquainted with these personalities from the past. I had always heard we were related to Davy Crockett, as my grandmother was a Crockett, but what I didn't know was our connection to Col. Joseph Crockett, who served alongside Gen. George Washington during the Revolutionary War. He was my great-great-great-great-grandfather, which made me a Daughter of the American Revolution. This one piece of information set my mind whirling. I had uncovered some rich family history I had known very little about because the knowledge of it sat in boxes for years. But just because I didn't know about it didn't mean it wasn't true.

This got me thinking about a far more superior connection—our kingdom connection. We are a part of a revolution that's going on right now, one that brings rescue to the souls and minds of broken people. It's a spiritual advancement here on Earth that is unseen. It is neither limited to a particular area of the world nor bound by time. On the contrary, it was—and is—thriving. We may have been Christians for years and never realized the depth of our active kinship to this sacred dominion. We are Daughters of a Kingdom Revolution, one that is taking the world by storm.

Consider how the scriptures describe our current heavenly connection:

But you have come to Mount Zion, to the city of the living God, the heavenly Jerusalem. You have come to thousands upon thousands of angels in joyful assembly. (Hebrews 12:22)

Delving into *whatever is true* unpacks our sacred association to God's kingdom. We have a rich spiritual ancestry that is not meant to sit in boxes for years or to be read as fables from the past. The revolutionary leader of our souls wants to open our eyes to the green pastures of our kingdom connection and to the unique purpose for which He placed us in this world right now, today.

So, let's begin the unpacking. There is an expansive kinship that God wants the eyes of our hearts to look at, but we need to back up a bit to see it. Here is what I mean. Naturally, as humans, we get caught up in the proximity of our agenda—our next plan, our current struggle, what we need to stop doing or start doing, and so on. It is the weight of the temporal. That's why my boxes sat unopened for so many years. What we really need to do is ask ourselves why. Why do we do the things we do and make the choices we make day after day? Throughout history, we see God calling His people to an eternal perspective, to look at the bigger picture and consider the why. And with this comes the weight of light.

Becoming acquainted with faith-filled souls from scripture helps brings this type of illumination to our pilgrimage. In referring to these biblical saints in his book *The Pursuit of God*, A. W. Tozer says, "Come near to the holy men and women of the past and you will soon feel the heat of their desire after God. They mourned for him, they prayed and wrestled and sought for him day and night in season and out, and when they had found him, the finding was all the sweeter for the long seeking." And it's not just biblical figures who inspire us but our historical Christian ancestors as well. The Luthers and Augustines, the Spurgeons and Wesleys, the Alcotts and Muellers, the Ten Booms, the Carmichaels, and the Elliots—all their stories help us uncover a vibrant spiritual heritage that holds clues to our own purpose. It flips on the light switch so we can see the panoramic picture of God's larger plan for our lives.

Esther is one of those people. In her earthly journey, we see a great example of the weight and power of the unseen kingdom light. A product of a rich spiritual heritage, Esther was a Jewess with the birth name of Hadassah. Although she was orphaned, Hadassah was trained in deep spiritual truths by her cousin Mordecai. She was no stranger to broken circumstances, having been a part of an exiled people-group from her earliest years. This did not stop her cousin from instilling the truth of the promise to which she belonged. Despite how everything appeared in Hadassah's broken environment, there was another world—the bigger picture of a spiritual heritage—that Mordecai faithfully pointed her to. As light reflects off an object to create sight, we can see that Mordecai was reflecting the weight of God's truth into Hadassah's life. Even while living among nonbelievers and being exposed to the reigning culture of darkness, Mordecai delivered daily doses of light to Hadassah.

As we examine our own lives, we must ask ourselves some questions. What light sources are reflecting truth to our minds? Do we have something or someone like Mordecai reflecting deep revelations of light into our hearts? This is an important aspect of our journey to consider. Whom do we allow into our inner circle of influence?

For various reasons, we often make the mistake of seeking spiritual guidance or direction from people who do not point us to the light. Maybe it's because they are close to us, or perhaps they are considered wise. But if they do not project this kind of light, or they are not in tune with the truth of God's active spiritual kingdom and our connection to it, we are vulnerable to their inability to see the bigger picture.

Besides spiritually minded friends, truth and the reality of God's presence can come from many sources: digging into the Bible, a kind act from a stranger, the teaching of a spiritual leader, the wisdom from a book, a quiet time in prayer, inspirational meditations, or a quiet walk in nature.

With that in mind, let's think about this more deeply. What keeps us far from truth, and what draws us near to it? What in our life creates space for God to shine His light through the shadows of our minds to illuminate the gaze of the soul? I'm not talking about just good theology but rather the sweet presence of the sacred light of Jesus and the greater purposes of His kingdom.

In his book *The Pursuit of God*, A. W. Tozer eloquently describes his quest for the kind of truth that stirs the soul: "If a man has only correct doctrine to offer me, I am sure to slip out at the first intermission to seek the company of someone who has seen for himself how lovely is the face of Him who is the Rose of Sharon and the Lily of the Valley. Such a man can help me, and no one else."

Tozer was in search of something greater than protocol and orthodoxy; he was looking for a kingdom connection of an experiential nature.

Back to the story of Esther in the Bible. Before she was taken to be groomed for her introduction to the king, her cousin Mordecai gave her the new name of Esther, which means, among other things, "hiddenness." Here we gain insight into a bigger plan for Esther's life. Though she lived in the darkness that engulfed the Persian Empire, her true identity was hidden with God and His kingdom. It was this very light (the Hadassah hidden in Esther) that pierced the darkness in a grand event of unstoppable magnitude.

It is interesting that scripture also describes our relationship to Christ as one of hiddenness:

For you died to this life, and your real life is hidden with Christ in God. (Colossians 3:3)

As we ponder the deeper meaning of Esther's life, we gain profound insight into our own spiritual lives. There is something greater and with eternal qualities that we, too, are a part of. We walk about a world that is perpetually under a cloak of darkness because Satan is the ruler of this world, but our true identity is hidden in the light of Christ and His spiritual kingdom.

Considering Esther's new position as queen, we can perceive opposing weights at work. A weight of darkness began to masquerade as light, a false light that was temporal, but it seemed more relevant and visible than the true light of God. (This is always the case with that which is visibly secular.) Esther could see, hear, touch, and smell the luxuries and comforts of being a queen. The true light that once radiated from Mordecai's words was no longer present. Naturally, the weight of darkness shrouded the truth of God's promise to her and her people. The voice of her cousin Mordecai—which had served as a daily dose of light in her life and had so often redirected her priorities as a girl—had become distanced and dulled with the passage of time, and his once-unhindered access to his beloved Hadassah was now limited to messengers who communicated on his behalf to this now-exclusive queen. Walled in by the dark light of earthly royalty, Esther lost sight of her true self—the eternal royalty of being intricately connected to God's kingdom of light and truth, the hidden Hadassah part of Esther.

## Our part in the big picture

Just like Esther, we, too, have within us this hidden light that cannot be extinguished, this divine royalty of whatever is true. Even when we feel we've lost sight of ourselves and our purpose in Christ, the light is still there. We may be facing a season of great darkness, but the light remains infinitely more powerful. It does not matter how big our troubles or issues are—God is bigger. There is no changing this spiritual fact. Sometimes, we may not be aware of this reality because the truth is hidden. But remember: truth is real whether we see it or not.

To many Christians, this idea might seem strange because the concept of God's kingdom is often contemplated as a forthcoming event. To the secular person, however, the idea of a current spiritual reality is thrilling because of the intrinsic desire of every human heart to be a part of a present sacred realm. Concepts such as meditation, journey, path, enlightenment, pilgrimage, and inner peace all convey the yearning that exists in every human soul for a spiritual course to follow. Non-Christians who have a spiritual mind-set often possess an enviable dedication that many Christians lack.

As believers, we often find ourselves immersed in a language of theology that falls short of kingdom flavor and subdues our spiritual senses. When we're perfectly satisfied with concepts we can understand that are not over-spiritualized, our Christianity becomes more of a checklist of what we should or should not believe. As such, we miss out on the experiential side of the heavenly sphere that sparkles and shines all around us.

We may never have realized just how much God desires His children to be consciously in touch with their connection to an eternal kingdom in a current and active sense. For instance, take a closer look at the following verses from Ephesians, particularly the wording of the last phrase:

> Because of his great love for us, God, who is rich in mercy, made us alive with Christ even when we were dead in our transgressions—it's by grace you have been saved. God raised us up with Christ and seated us with him in the heavenly realm in Christ Jesus. (Ephesians 2:4–6)

In this scripture, we see the compelling present reality of God's kingdom. Our position in that kingdom is operating from a real-time presence with Christ. If we have thought the term *heavenly realm* implied a vague afterlife somewhere in the sky, we've been mistaken.

The same was true with Esther. She might have been inclined to think that Mordecai's teachings were far removed from her reality as queen and were meant for another time and place. But she, like us, was part of a current and ongoing invisible kingdom of people who were (and are) very real. Her story reflected the truth of a Savior who would be the rescuer of this people-group through grace, giving them citizenship with an eternal purpose to flourish here on Earth. Likewise, our life is hidden in Christ and connected to this spiritual realm even though we are wrapped in the world and engulfed in a temporary weight of darkness.

Throughout the Bible, we see our covenant connection with God. Jesus personified this truth when He said, "My kingdom is not of this world" (John 18:36). The book of Hebrews spotlights regular people like you and me who were called to represent this heavenly realm on Earth. For instance, Moses forsook the treasures of Egypt to be connected to his people-group of spiritual kind. When warned about things not seen, Noah, in holy fear, built an ark to save his family, who were part of this kingdom presence on Earth. Abraham made his home in a foreign country because he was looking forward to the city whose architect and builder is God. We also have a role in this larger flow. We, too, are part of this bigger picture, this heavenly realm that is on the forefront and cannot be thwarted. Embracing this sacred eternal connection brings a stunningly fresh view of *whatever is true.*

*Questions to Ponder:*

1.  When thinking about Christian figures from the past (biblical or historical), who inspires you, and why?
2.  Can you think of a few people you would consider placing in your inner circle of influence? Whom would you remove?
3.  Can you recall a time when you were made aware that you are part of a bigger plan or purpose?

# Whatever Is True
## Part Three

——∽——

ONSIDER THIS QUOTE BY A. W. Tozer: "A spiritual kingdom lies all about us, embracing us, altogether within reach of our inner selves, waiting for us to recognize it. God Himself is here awaiting our response to His presence. This eternal world will come alive to us the moment we begin to reckon upon its reality." Does this excite your soul? Does it enliven your spiritual senses? If so, there is good reason. As we become increasingly aware of God's kingdom, we become spiritually invigorated and impassioned.

No wonder Stephen, one of the apostles of the early church, was able to experience a deadly stoning while simultaneously praising God. His life is a perfect example of how the weightier the spiritual kingdom reality becomes, the less the disappointments of this world lay hold of our hearts. One reality overcomes the other. That which is unshakable becomes brighter and more alive, and that which is fleeting becomes dimmer and less seizing to the soul. This reminds me of the words in the old hymn by Hellen Lemmel:

Turn your eyes upon Jesus,
Look full in His wonderful face,
And the things of earth will grow strangely dim,
In the light of His glory and grace.

What about you? Is something other than truth seizing your thoughts and framing your perspective? If we don't cultivate spiritual vision, our thinking will seize up with whatever our minds are full of. Think about this in relation to your life. What is stealing your time, maybe even years, and holding you captive? No matter how inviting it may seem or how big it looms in your life, it's only a shadow—it's not the light. Perhaps it's time to stop staring at it as if it were the light. Our minds are meant to soar into the marvels of the spiritual realm. But as long as they are full of temporal perspectives and pursuits, darkness is inevitable.

If Stephen had valued this world more highly than the heavenly realm, he would not have been able to see the beauty of the heavenly kingdom God was pleased to reveal to him. The greater force of light burst through the dark clouds of persecution. Right in the middle of Stephen being stoned, the Lord opened a window and allowed him to peer with his physical eyes at that which was spiritual. "Look! I see the heavens opened and the Son of Man standing at the right hand of God!" (Acts 7:56). This passage reveals that God loves to make the kingdom manifest to those who seek it. But when we get caught up in the weight of thinking that veils this truth, we miss out on the amazing venture meant for us—namely, being seated with Christ in the heavenly realm while living in the earthly realm. Simply put, there is a real community and kingdom that God desires us to actively be a part of—even now.

Scripture is replete with the subject of the kingdom of God being near at hand. In Matthew 4:23, Jesus's ministry is described in terms of preaching the gospel of the kingdom: "And he went throughout all Galilee, teaching in their synagogues and proclaiming the gospel of the kingdom…"

We may have never recognized the recurring theme of the kingdom as God intended it, meaning right here with us, right now. But once we're attuned to it, we can barely turn a page in the New Testament without reading a reference to it. We see it in Jesus's commission to His disciples when He "sent them out to proclaim the kingdom of God" (Luke 9:2). In Jesus's counsel regarding their physical necessities, we are told, "Instead, seek His kingdom, and these things will be added to you" (Luke 12:3).

Journeying with the ability to see spiritually is the exciting pilgrimage we make when connected to this sacred realm. We once viewed life in one way, but now with the help of the Holy Spirit, we have the ability to view it in another—with a divine lens—one that is able to take in light and see remarkable sights because we have been raised to newness of life under the illumination of Jesus Christ. Why would we allow our souls to travel through life without pursuing the spiritual mind's ability to see in this way? Yet many Christians remain in the dark about this. They do not recognize they are part of something bigger, a vibrant spiritual family that expands in space and time. They separate the spiritual from the secular and are unaware of their royal heritage while traveling Earth. When they hear of it, it seems more like a beautiful story from another time, like a fairy tale. But the truth is, the kingdom of God is perpetually present and surrounding us, and we are its inhabitants.

Let's consider how scripture describes our citizenship in this dominion:

> Consequently, you are no longer foreigners and strangers, but fellow citizens with God's people and also members of his household. (Ephesians 2:19)

Before we can comprehend the magnitude of the kingdom of heaven, we must first understand that Jesus Christ is the kingdom entrance and the One Pearl of Great Price on which the entire foundation of this kingdom rests, "built on the foundation of the apostles and prophets, with Christ Jesus himself as the chief cornerstone" (Ephesians 2:20). Jesus aligns all facts and accounts accurately with the truth of this great and mysterious realm. We see early reference to King Jesus, as well as the two opposing weights of light and darkness, when God speaks to the serpent after Adam and Eve's fall from grace in the Garden of Eden:

> I will put enmity between you and the woman, and between your offspring and her offspring; he shall bruise your head, and you shall bruise his heel. (Genesis 3:15)

Notice that the *offspring* here, explained as the singular *He* that was to bruise the head of Satan, is none other than Jesus. This verse implies that Jesus would come as the originator of an entire group of people.

The plural *offspring* (us) through Christ is seen in God's promise to Abraham in the foretelling of this kingdom of people in Genesis 17:7. Then, again in the New Testament, scripture says that those who put their faith in Jesus will be considered heirs and offspring of Abraham:

> And if you are Christ's, then you are Abraham's offspring, heirs according to the promise. (Galatians 3:29)

This is true not just for Jews, for whom this passage was originally written, but for all who believe:

> Gentiles are fellow heirs, members of the same body, and partakers of the promise in Christ Jesus through the gospel. (Ephesians 3:6)

It is evident that this kingdom filled with the offspring from this One Seed, Jesus, currently represents the light in this world. All of life points to this wonderful truth of God establishing a beautiful and diversified people-group for Himself through Jesus Christ.

We must realize, however, that being a part of this kingdom will cause us to encounter two principles throughout our life: light and darkness. The light will reveal the kingdom to our hearts, whereas the darkness will always try to conceal it. Therefore, while in our temporal bodies, we will experience a recurring cycle of light, darkness, and a return to light again. This pattern follows our earthly journey from beginning to end.

This cycle began when God created us and placed us in the Garden of Eden in communion with Himself in perfect light—the moment of creation. The cycle continued when Satan came along and cast a shadow that caused a separation in our communion with God, and we became darkened—the moment of Adam and Eve's fall from grace. The cycle came full circle when Jesus rescued us through His work on the cross to bring us back into the light of fellowship with Him—the moment of redemption.

Understanding this cycle will help us recognize the recurring conflict of it in our thinking. This ongoing struggle can be felt in the weight of light granted to our resurrected souls and the weight of darkness that continually tries to block that light from our minds.

Satan wants to keep truth covered in darkness. There is so much abundance to be had in this new and present kingdom, and he would like nothing better than to waste our days as Christians stuck in the temporary, trivial, broken mind-set of the realm we have been transferred out of.

This explains why to the degree the kingdom of heaven is illuminated in our hearts, its presence is felt even though it is fully and indisputably around us. In other words, if we don't press into the kingdom with our spiritual senses, we tend to forget it's there. We fall prey to spiritual amnesia as we get caught up in worldly concerns—that is, until the light breaks through our darkened clouds and shines once again. When that happens, we recognize a bigger picture, and we are reassured once again that we are not alone and that the angels and a multitude of heavenly participants are cheering us on. People such as Esther are in this rooting section, having already made their earthly pilgrimage.

Do you have relatives who have passed from this earthly life and now live in heaven? They, too, along with other Christians who have gone before us, are collectively a part of the big story, a part of our spiritual genealogy. They have a great interest in seeing us press through the dark cycles of our lives into the light. We can catch a glimpse of the marvelous truth of their presence in this scripture:

> Therefore, since we are surrounded by such a great cloud of witnesses, let us throw off everything that hinders and the sin that so easily entangles. And let us run with perseverance the race marked out for us. (Hebrews 12:1)

This big-picture view will cause *whatever is true* to emerge with great brilliance. This is what Mordecai's news did for Esther. Remember his words to her?

> Do not think that because you are in the king's house you alone of all the Jews will escape. For if you remain silent at this time, relief and

deliverance for the Jews will arise from another place, but you and your father's family will perish. And who knows but that you have come to your royal position for such a time as this. (Esther 4:13, 14)

Wow, talk about clarity! Esther was not only given a view of the bigger picture, she was given a view of the impact *she* was designed to have in light of the big picture. Mordecai was saying to Esther that she needed to consider that God had put her in this position for a reason other than what she thought—a reason that had eternal purpose—and that she was connected to a people-group who had come before her and would go on long after her.

It is the same for us. When we look at everything in our temporal realm from an eternal vantage point, our view becomes divinely comprehensive. We consider what God might be doing in our lives, and we realize that we are part of a bigger plan. When we are too close to the earthly situation, we can see only a partial picture, which makes our minds vulnerable to all sorts of shadows and weights of darkness. That's where we tend to dwell and focus our thoughts.

Mordecai's words were life giving to Esther. It caused the weight in her mind to shift from below to above. As Esther's lens widened, her view encompassed the larger overarching perspective of a heavenly realm that she was intricately a part of, and the light of truth burst forth!

## Spiritual sight rescues us

What is the bigger picture for you as it pertains not only to God's plan for your life but also to what that means in the big scheme of God's rescue of your mind? How will this influence your participation in the kingdom, even now? Surely, it would be a great time to let the Author of your salvation begin a rewrite of your thought-life based on whatever is true. Grasping the bigger spiritual story of our temporal station in this life transforms our thinking.

For example, consider the common struggle of inadequacy, or the feeling of being insufficient or incapable or having no great value. This emotion holds a weight of darkness that easily cloaks our sight. The antidote is the heavy weight of divine illumination. The truth is that we are more of an integral part of spiritual activities here on Earth than we may have recognized.

The Lord's Prayer is one of the most powerful examples of this reality. In "thy kingdom come, thy will be done on Earth as it is in heaven," we are reminded that we are the kingdom remnant of light that walks about the earth. The word done can be translated "form". We are part of the people-group of God in this era on the timeline of history forming and shaping His kingdom upon this planet.

This counteracts feelings of inadequacy in a radical way. It shifts the weight in our minds from thinking we are of no value to recognizing we actually have significant value—divine value. It turns the light switch on to help us realize that in God's bigger plan, we are "valuable" heavenly contributors during our earthly lives. We may be the only encounter with the kingdom of God that a stranger has in his or her day. Once the eyes of our hearts take in this truth, light beams will cast new and confident direction on our daily path. Grasping God's otherworldly design—that He has placed us in this life to be a part of the heavenly realm here on Earth—fills us with sacred purpose.

If, however, we continue to think our inadequacies make us less valuable, which is what Satan wants us to think, a variety of false ideas will darken our path. We may shrink back from opportunities, become neutralized and ineffective, fall into unhealthy relationships, and potentially make destructive life choices. Satan's strategy from the beginning of time has been to spin false and darkened ideas that will cast a shadow on whatever is true, giving us a myopic view to keep us stuck in the ruts of broken and hopeless thinking.

To live in a kingdom reality with a kingdom mind-set, we need to step out of the shadows and renew our thoughts daily with God's eternal truth. Remember, the ongoing conflict between light and dark—and its recurring cycle—remains in our lives as long as we dwell in our earthly bodies. We will wake up every day with the mounting weight of the world trying to pin us down and make us forget about our kingdom connection. Insecurities, doubt, anxieties, inferiorities, and inadequacies are crouching at our door in the shadow of darkness. Sometimes, even success is vying for our attention, keeping us from a greater purpose.

It is our default nature as humans to live in the temporal. This is part of living in a broken world. The only thing that can shift this weight is saturating our thinking with whatever is true.

When we believe we are connected to something bigger and more purposeful than the difficulty or temptation we are facing, there is no room for insecurity or inadequacy to take root in us. We belong to a kingdom full of light, one that uses even our brokenness and inabilities as an avenue for God to shine forth His divine capabilities. In fact, this is the structure of His new kingdom. It is empowering to consider. The truth is that His glory emits unobstructed brilliance through our cracked clay jars of human frailty. Embracing this weight of light will cause the dark shadows to dispel. Even in our weakness, He is able. It is His specialty. In Christ, there is victory in brokenness.

My grace is sufficient for you, for My power is perfected in weakness. (2 Corinthians 12:10)

As we bring this chapter to an end, we draw the parallel of the much-awaited Christ, who was looked down on by His own people and found inadequate as Messiah. They were looking for an assertive and able leader riding on a lofty warhorse. But instead, a gentle and humble man of carpenter status arrived on a mild donkey. The very people awaiting His arrival were disappointed. Yet Christ did not waver in His message or His ministry depending on their sentiments. He did not make room in His heart for feelings of inadequacy. He knew who He was, He knew the kingdom He belonged to, and He knew His value. Jesus framed His identity through His Father's eyes.

The people's expectations cast a dark shadow to their own detriment, which blocked them from seeing the truth that was right in front of them. The servant leadership of our Lord was inadequate by man's flawed standards; they didn't even see His might or power even though many marveled at His miracles. However, in the greatest act of strength of all time, He subjected Himself to be crucified.

For he was crucified in weakness, but lives by the power of God.
(2 Corinthians 13:4)

His way was meek and therefore found wanting by the world's standards. We must now look intently to this Rock from which we were hewn. The Redeemer, the Stone the builders rejected, became the cornerstone of the most exquisite countercultural domain—a royal kingdom that we are all intricately and currently a part of. Like Esther, we may feel distanced from the truth as it applies to our own value. But the Hadassah part of our lives, which is hidden in Christ, will continue to flourish. "He who began a good work will carry it on to completion" (Philippians 1:6). Though it be shrouded in the weight of darkness of this era—or in personal brokenness and sin—or doubt and faithless seasons—or people's failed expectations—it is real and weighty with eternal purpose, full of light. God has set in motion, and it cannot be thwarted.

In the following chapters, we will highlight several women of the Bible, including Hannah, Ruth, Rebekah, Abigail, and Sarah. Looking at their stories will help us see that we are part of something bigger than we may have realized. They are sisters, daughters, mothers, and grandmothers, and all of us together are one big family of kingdom people. Tuck this verse deep in your heart, and let it water your soul and bring daily doses of light to your mind:

But you are a chosen people, a royal priesthood, a holy nation, God's special possession, that you may declare the praises of him who called you out of darkness into his wonderful light. (1 Peter 2:9)

*Questions to Ponder:*

1. What temporal circumstance seems to seize your thoughts, even though you know it's a shadow?
2. How can looking at your life circumstance in light of the bigger picture change your perspective?

3. Does that give you an eternal perspective and infuse you with confidence? How would you describe the difference?

# CHAPTER 3

## Whatever Is Honorable
## Part One

⟶

I MAGINE YOU ARE IN BEAUTIFUL, breathtaking Bali. A journey of thousands of miles has brought you to an ancient retreat center far from the cares of the world. You are here to listen to the words of a well-known Christian sage who is nothing short of brilliant. Ushered into a large meeting space with a few hundred other eager visitors, you are filled with excitement. As you glance around, you notice that everyone looks breathless with anticipation. You can hear only a few faint sounds of coughing, but other than that, it is so silent you could hear a pin drop. A still sense of awe fills the space. You are struck with wonder at the grandness of the moment.

The speaker makes his way to the center of the room. Instead of his typical discourse, he announces that he is going to invite one person from the crowd for an impromptu interview. An attendant rushes over with two folding chairs—one for him and one for his interviewee. A name is called, and it's yours! You can hardly move at first, you're so stunned. Feeling surreal, you stand and walk toward the teacher, with trembling legs. He greets you with a firm, comforting handshake and urges you to ask anything you like. You spend the next hour nervously yet eagerly posing as many questions concerning the issues in your life as you can think of. He answers each one patiently and with deep and profound wisdom.

Of course this narrative is fictional, but there is still a sense of wonder in considering the excitement of such an experience. If you took careful notice of our story, you may have even caught the heightened point of awe at the moment of silence—a silence so still that you might have heard a pin drop. This was intentional to set the stage for our next focus phrase: *whatever is honorable.*

The word *honorable* in the original Greek language of the New Testament has the meaning of "inspiring reverence." When the Bible talks about having a fear of the Lord, it is referring to this kind of encounter, one in which awe is felt in such a deep part of the heart that it hushes all other distractions. Although our opening story conveys a certain level of wonder, it's nothing compared to the direct access we actually *do* have to the true and living God! Imagine Jesus pulled up a seat for you and said, "Ask whatever you like." We may never have considered this in such personal terms, but this kind of direct access is part of our kingdom reality.

Consider what Moses must have felt when he came face to face with the burning bush. Remember how he was told to take off his shoes? It wasn't that the physical ground itself was special, but rather that he was standing in the presence of the Holy Trinity. It was sacred space. God was showcasing for Moses His masterful design of redemption, which included all three members of the God-head: the Father displayed the work of the Son (represented in the thorn bush), who would take on the curse of humanity, and the Holy Spirit (represented in the fire) would raise Him from death, forever lifting the curse. What a wonder to behold.

Now consider this. That one awe-inspiring moment in Moses's life can be an everyday opportunity for the Christian. Because of Jesus's work on the cross, we have direct access to the Father, Son, and Holy Spirit each moment of our lives. We don't have to travel thousands of miles to come into the presence of this triune Counselor. Even on the stormiest of days or in the darkest of nights, blue skies can open up to His magnificent presence. And when they do, we recognize that we are standing on holy ground.

In fact, it would serve our hearts well to take off our shoes, so to speak, as we journey deeper into understanding the rescue that God provides for our thinking. Not only has Jesus lifted the curse on our souls, but by the power of the Holy Spirit, He is at work lifting the curse from our minds. The Trinity, three holy persons in one, works on our behalf, with each having different but equally important roles in the redemption of our thinking. As we mine for riches in our new focus phrase, *whatever is honorable*, we can think of it this way: we must set our minds on whatever inspires the "wow" of God.

## Spiritual hearing

In the previous chapters, we talked about the weight of broken thinking that burdens our minds and blocks us from healthy spiritual thinking. We discussed weight in terms of light and its effect on our spiritual sight. In this chapter, we will look at weight in relation to our spiritual ability to hear from the heart, where keen attentiveness to the triune presence is cultivated. Like the whistling of a bird that might go unnoticed unless we incline our ears, for the Christian, the spiritual sense of hearing opens the mind to new wonders daily.

But what keeps us from hearing spiritually? What in our lives is upstaging the sounds of the sacred? Whether it is pools of broken thinking or the heavy weight of the temporary things of life, the boisterous noise of the world blocks our ability to hear the gentle leading of our Savior. Consider the following scripture, and take particular notice of Elijah's reaction:

> The LORD said, "Go out and stand on the mountain in the presence of the LORD, for the LORD is about to pass by." Then a great and powerful wind tore the mountains apart and shattered the rocks before the LORD, but the LORD was not in the wind. After the wind there was an earthquake, but the LORD was not in the earthquake. After the earthquake came a fire, but the LORD was not in the fire. And after the fire came a gentle whisper. When Elijah heard it, he pulled his cloak over his face and went out and stood at the mouth of the cave. (1 Kings 19:11–13)

A contrast is deliberately laid out for us here. We often see this theme in scripture where the bold is presented first, only to have the meek and less assuming emerge victorious. In this verse, the powerful forces of nature boomed, but it was in the gentle whisper where God chose to reveal Himself. Angels are often portrayed covering their faces in the Lord's presence as a token of reverence, but here we get a glimpse of the same kind of awed reaction in the man Elijah. His response is a snapshot of human reverence toward a divine God.

The whisper of the Lord speaks mighty things to the soul. We must listen with intent and dial down the weighty noise levels of our lives to hear the Lord speaking to us. That means making conscious efforts to disconnect from the loud demands on our attention—including our own broken thinking. Whether it's the torrential winds of success, the quaking of life's trials and tribulations, or the fire of all-consuming emotions, all must give way to the gentle sound of quiet.

Venturing into the realm of God's truth and light, we search for patches of sacred silence where we may find stillness and thereby hear the tender whispers of God. Oh, how we need it. It's a place of sweet meditation and contemplation, a holy ground untouched by the weight of darkness and the noise of this world. Some even suggest that this is the surest posture of the heart to carry our prayers, as on wings. Tim Keller says, "The Holy Spirit himself preaches here."

As God's children, we recognize His voice, but only if we are listening. If we are, then deep inside our hearts we will discern the Savior's leading.

This is what Jesus alludes to when He says that our hearts are His temple:

Don't you know that you yourselves are God's temple and that God's Spirit dwells in your midst? (1 Corinthians 3:16)

We are His sacred dwelling place, and He tabernacles with us. This is an incredible change from over two thousand years ago, when only the high priest was allowed to enter the temple's holiest place. He was the intercessor who offered sacrifices on behalf of the sins of the people. He alone was able to access the Holy of Holies where the Lord dwelt in glory, and only once a year. How mind boggling to consider that God calls our very hearts His temple. His presence is a near and personal reality. The vast grandness of God comes to us intimately through Jesus Christ in the closest-possible proximity—our hearts.

## Approaching God

When we recognize that our ability to approach the living God in such a personal manner is part of the bigger plan discussed in chapter 2, it inspires a sense of awe in us. The baby Jesus, who was prophesied in Isaiah 7, was God, who, by His Spirit, would tabernacle with us (notice the Trinity). Matthew 1:23 says, "Look! The virgin will conceive a child! She will give birth to a son, and they will call him Immanuel, which means 'God is with us.'" It was a plan set in motion long before the ages, culminating in Jesus sacrificing His life as atonement for our sins. He became the high priest of a new covenant sealed with His own blood, thereby replacing the old priestly system. Scripture tells us that in the moment of His death, the veil in the temple was torn from top to bottom. Because of His sacrifice, the very veil that kept us out of the Holy of Holies was opened so that we may enter into the very presence of the Holy One.

> This hope we have as an anchor of the soul, a hope both sure and steadfast and one which enters within the veil, where Jesus has entered as a forerunner for us, having become a high priest forever according to the order of Melchizedek. (Hebrews 6:19–20)

Our spiritual ancestors from long ago did not have the access to God that we have today. But like us, they had an intrinsic desire to draw near to Him. We can see this in the Old Testament when Hannah entered the temple and poured out her heart to God. Of course she was not allowed in the Holy of Holies but was in the courts in full force with her prayers and petitions to gain the closest-possible contact. Whatever was the protocol made no difference to her. She silenced propriety for the sake of intimacy, longing to hear from the

Lord personally. The priest in the temple that day, Eli, was shocked by her departure from tradition.

You see, Hannah's husband, Elkanah, had two wives. She was highly favored by her husband, but she was unable to conceive. Elkanah's other wife bore him multiple children, and Hannah was tormented by this woman who taunted her for being childless. Hannah knew her only hope to open her womb lay in God and His ability. On this particular occasion, while in the temple, she laid out her pain—not before the priest, as was the custom, but before God.

Hannah's story illustrates a truth: when we silence the outer noise of our lives, our inner pleas toward God become loud with urgency. The Good Shepherd's voice, heard as a whisper, is often ushered in by desperation and desire—begging, to be exact. This is what the priest observed in Hannah's supplications before the Lord in the temple that day.

We may not realize the important role that begging has in our dealings with the Lord. In the Sermon on the Mount (Matthew 5), Jesus confirms this when He teaches that those who are needy (poor) of heart are blessed. In fact, the Greek lexicon describes the word *poor* as a kind of poverty that can be helped only by begging. This same meaning is conveyed when Jesus says, "Ask and it will be given to you" (Matthew 7:7). The word *ask* in this usage (in the original Greek) means "to beg." Beggars recognize the desperate state of their need.

When we are empty of our own ability, we understand that our rescue must come from another source. This propels our hearts toward God, and when we turn to Him, we are blessed.

Hannah begged the Lord with such intensity that the priest mistook her behavior for drunkenness:

> Now Eli the priest was sitting on a chair by the doorpost of the LORD's temple. In bitterness of soul, Hannah wept much and prayed to the LORD. And she made a vow, saying, "O LORD Almighty, if you will only look upon your servant's misery and remember me, and

not forget your servant but give her a son, then I will give him to the LORD for all the days of his life, and no razor will ever be used on his head." As she kept on praying to the LORD, Eli observed her mouth. Hannah was praying in her heart, and her lips were moving, but her voice was not heard.

Eli thought she was drunk and said to her, "How long will you keep on getting drunk? Get rid of your wine."

"Not so, my lord," Hannah replied. "I am a woman who is deeply troubled. I have not been drinking wine or beer; I was pouring out my soul to the LORD. Do not take your servant for a wicked woman; I have been praying here out of my great anguish and grief."

Eli answered, "Go in peace, and may the God of Israel grant you what you have asked of him."

She said, "May your servant find favor in your eyes." Then she went her way and ate something, and her face was no longer downcast. (1 Samuel 1:9–18)

Eli was initially shocked. He was not accustomed to seeing such a display of emotion. Yet Hannah was so deeply engrossed in pouring out her heart to God like a pauper that she didn't even think about how it might look to someone on the outside of that encounter. She was on a mission to get alone with God in sacred silence, and she was loud with earnestness that dialed down the world's impression of her. It is interesting to note that in such a time, when the priestly system was in place, Hannah chose to take her need directly to the Lord. This was especially unusual for a woman of that culture.

As Christians, we have direct access to God, but we often seek other voices of counsel and reassurance. We have made for ourselves many priests, in a manner of speaking. We look outside the veil to heal our heartaches, and we are driven to worldly, temporal solutions. Although it is important to have a safe circle of people in our lives, approaching God first in the privacy of beggarly prayers is a critical habit to establish. In doing so, we find that He moves in ways we might otherwise miss.

*God does not turn away from neediness*

Hannah exhibited an excessive sense of need in her desire to have a baby. In fact, the people who knew her might have labeled her needy. In today's world, neediness has taken on a negative connotation. As a result, we may feel compelled to combat neediness with self-help practices. As confidence-building as this may seem, it actually leads us farther from a reverence of God. The truth is when we recognize our deep need and God's ability to meet our need. That's when we are best positioned to experience the "wow" of God.

We all struggle with being in need on some level. From the moment we are born, we are in need of reconciliation to Christ. But because we reach out to the wrong sources for help and healing, we become broken and bruised. Over time, the weight of neediness manifests itself in an excessive drive for affection, attention, and reassurance. For people who struggle with neediness, feeling secure is fleeting. Even when we're affirmed, we continue to feel an overwhelming anxiety to have these needs met again and again. There are multiple reasons that neediness is more present in some than in others. It could be anything from disposition, compulsion, to emotional deprivation. Even if we have been given indulgent nurturing, the result may be the same: an excessive sense of need.

For Hannah, there were a number of contributing factors. She lived in a culture where being a fulfilled and happy woman meant having children, and she was barren. On top of this, she was antagonized by another woman who was bearing the children of her husband. This dynamic was an unhealthy contributing factor to her heightened sense of neediness. She simply did not feel reassured by her mate, no matter how much he told her he loved her. We can observe her husband's frustration in his response to her sorrow: "Hannah, why are you weeping? Why don't you eat? Why are you downhearted? Don't I mean more to you than ten sons?" (1 Samuel 1:8). Hannah was inconsolable because of her desperate sense of need that even her husband could not fulfill.

We may never have thought about it this way, but neediness is internally loud, and it becomes externally loud when we press to get our needs met by other people. That's because the beggarly cry in our hearts (that is meant only for God) manifests itself in clinginess and desperation. You may have observed a needy person entering a room, only to have others walk the other direction to avoid contact. Those who struggle with neediness notice that the people around them pull away as expectations become too all consuming. The pattern of relationships that crumble due to this struggle is recognizable. But the needy person internalizes it as rejection, which further compounds the need for affirmation. Because neediness never rests, it often leaves us with feelings of emptiness. For those of us who struggle with neediness, it is not until we come to this place as Hannah did in recognizing that the only hope for our dark clouds of neediness are the blue skies of accessing God directly.

Are there areas in your life where you recognize a sense of need that pulls you in unhealthy directions or compels you toward inappropriate behaviors in an effort to get those needs met? Are you searching for voices of reassurance in earthly "priests"? If you are, be encouraged; recognizing this tendency is the first step toward redirecting and shifting weight to the divine.

Cultivating a new pattern of going directly to God will hush the loud cries in our hearts that urge us to extract reassurance from others. Being beggarly postured before our triune God silences the distractions that block our ability to hear His gentle leading. Remember, the only confidence we need comes from the Lord Jesus who is our High Priest, superior in every way.

*Questions to Ponder:*

1. The ability to hear the still, quiet voice of the Lord comes through the silencing of worldly distractions. Can you identify a time when you felt the presence of God in a way that inspired awe?
2. What part has begging played in your relationship with God? Can you recall a time when you begged before the Lord?
3. Can you identify where you try to get your needs met outside of God, or the ways you try to extract reassurance from others?

# Whatever Is Honorable
## Part Two

⟶ formative ⟵

THE VOICE OF THE LORD is a powerful thing. With words, God spoke the heavens into being. He merely said, "Let there be," and there was. By saying, "Be still," Jesus calmed the storm, and all was quiet again.

In his book *The Pursuit of God*, A. W. Tozer states, "The voice of God is the most powerful force in nature, for all energy is here only because the power-filled Word is being spoken." But the Bible is also clear about the human voice and the power it wields: "Life and death are in the power of the tongue" (Proverbs 18:21). Our words can build others up, but they can also tear others down. They can encourage, but they can also discourage. They can set free, but they can also burden. They can affirm, but they can also condemn.

The words we speak to ourselves can do the same thing. And when they are negative, loud, and intrusive, we are unable to hear spiritually. I'm talking about those thoughts that stay in our minds, the ones that linger or play like a reel over and over:

You have no worth.
You must prove yourself.
Your value is found in your body image.
Nobody cares.
You are alone.

You are a failure.

Other people's negative opinions of you must be true.

You are weird, and nobody wants to be your friend.

Our daily intake of negativity can't be measured because it's so constant, and the buildup of heaviness that weighs down our souls is more burdensome than we realize.

Let's consider a simple thought, such as "My weakness makes me feel like a failure." It turns us inward and does more harm than we realize. It comes easily because we are broken thinkers by nature. But the Lord has not left us without a solution for this problem. When we see this happening, we are to intercept, to "take captive every thought to make it obedient to Christ" (2 Corinthians 10:5).

But how do we do this?

Let me offer an illustration. Imagine a caricature of your face drawn on a piece of paper. Now imagine that you've drawn one thought bubble out to the side of your face (the left or right side) and another above your face. The one out to the side of your face represents your horizontal (secular) thoughts about your world, your life, and yourself. The one above your face represents your vertical thoughts—your conversations with God regarding the secular thinking going on in the other bubble.

Here is where the practical application comes in. If you talk with the Lord (engaging the spiritual bubble above your head) about your thoughts in the bubble next to your face (the secular bubble), your secular thinking will begin to change. For example, when put before the Lord, in the vertical thought bubble, the voice in your head that said "My weakness makes me feel like a failure" might change to "In my weakness, He is strong, and He doesn't turn away from my neediness." This simple practice of interception lifts the human spirit instantly and can help mold and shape kingdom thinking that is healthy and life giving.

Let's take a moment to think about these things. What is preoccupying your mind today? Are your thoughts turning back to one particular theme? Bring that thought before the Lord for discussion. Ask Him, "What do you think about this thought?" Or, "How should I think about that thought?" Take what the

Lord impresses on your heart and apply it to your secular thought bubble. This simple practice cultivates your spiritual listening skills. Speaking divine truths over our secular thoughts is a beautiful ongoing part of renewing the mind. It becomes a personal conversation between you and God and, eventually, your own thought-life. When we make room for a dialogue with God in this way, His Spirit refreshes our minds with His truth. We see an example of this in real application in Psalm 43:5 when the psalmist spoke to his own heart with God's truth:

> Why, my soul, are you downcast? Why so disturbed within me? Put your hope in God, for I will yet praise him, my Savior and my God. (Psalm 43:5)

## Meditation

As we continue our journey into the redemption of the mind, we find ourselves stepping into the wondrous reality of God's welcoming favor. God is never burdened or wearied by our pleas as people are. He understands our needs, even the things we think are needs but really are not. He longs to be a soothing balm and respite for our anxieties. It is a great comfort to realize God is not put off by our neediness, and He does turn away from us because of it. We can come to Him groveling, insecure, confused, and desperate, and His arms are always wide open.

It is not necessary to wait for mountaintop experiences of faith to pursue our triune God intimately. Cultivating a sense of His presence happens when we resolve to enter into a sacred space of silence, and we position ourselves in purposeful meditation. Philippians 4:8 sets the stage for this kind of spiritual experience. The phrase *think on these things* invites this divine encounter. Doing so will lead us into fresh opportunities for listening as we dial down the noise of the world, perhaps even gaining a different perspective on our circumstances.

The Lord desires to lead us to a place of intimate communion with Him that will open our eyes and ears to His kingdom presence. Fixing our minds on God, looking into the light of His truth, and listening for the movement of the Spirit is meditation at its finest.

Many Christians are afraid of the idea of meditation. This is because it is typically seen as a New Age practice, even though its origins are not secular. Meditation has been a means to ponder the thoughts of God since the beginning of time. We see it mentioned throughout the pages of scripture. In Genesis 24:63, we get a glimpse of Isaac meditating in the fields: "One evening as he was walking and meditating in the fields, he looked up and saw the camels coming." Jesus often found a quiet place to mediate and pray: "Very early in the morning, while it was still dark, Jesus withdrew to a solitary place to be alone with God and pray" (Mark 1:35). The Psalms talk about meditation continually. It was a regular practice among the men and women mentioned in the Old Testament, and even today, God uses our quiet moments of meditation to stir our hearts toward Him.

> They speak of the glorious splendor of your majesty—and I meditate on your wonderful works. (Psalm 145:5)

Meditation remains a beautiful spiritual activity intended for every believer. It is an enriching exercise for the soul. However, it is crucial for us to understand the difference between secular and sacred meditation. The key identifier will be whether we're centering our minds securely in the good news of the Gospel of Jesus Christ; otherwise, we may quickly find ourselves amiss.

By good news, I mean God's rescue plan for our souls, our hearts, and our minds.

Let me share a personal example from my own meditation time. I prepared my heart by asking the Spirit to reveal any weight or noise that might be holding me back and distracting me from His fullness. I intentionally dialed down my preoccupation with those thoughts. Because I was feeling anxious, I meditated on Psalm 23: "He lets me rest in green meadows; he leads beside peaceful streams." I can't think of a more serene location, so I began pondering what the scene might look like if I could peer into it. I imagined a meadow with balmy breezes gently blowing in waves and ripples. I could visualize small wildflowers moving to the rhythm of the wind. In my mind, I could also see the grass gently meeting the water's edge. This is when my meditation took a turn. All of a sudden, I imagined an alligator surfacing from the water. I felt alarmed that my meditation was interrupted by fearful thoughts. It wasn't until a few days later that it became clear what the trouble was. In Randy Alcorn's book *Heaven*, he says the following:

> The Bible promises us that one day, after the Resurrection, Heaven will be centered on the New Earth—the place where God's people will live forever. What are the implications of living on a transformed Earth? It means that we don't need to look up at the clouds to imagine Heaven; we simply need to look around us and imagine what all we see would be like without sin and death and suffering and corruption.

There it was—the good news of rescue! The secular scenario that had intruded into my meditation was anything but good news, and it caused anxiety. It needed to be taken captive and brought before the Lord. Psalm 23 is a picture of a divine setting—one that is free from the fear that is a part of the fallen world we live in now. It represents the kingdom we are currently connected to spiritually. It looks like the world God created in its original form before the fall—and will someday look after its restoration.

My heart thrilled at the thought of the sacredness of these verses. This is what my life looks like hidden in Him with no danger present—such a peaceful and tranquil place. I could linger in this blissful meadow for hours and days on end. All broken relationships would be mended. There would be no worries of darkness falling and danger looming. As I pondered this, I was quieted in my fears and anxieties. I became centered on that which is beyond the veil; that all this is possible because Christ died on the cross; that I, being subject to a cursed creation (Ephesians 2:23), have been made a partaker of this new kingdom. What an inspiring moment in pondering thoughts of the kingdom.

Meditation centers and aligns all thoughts to God and His master plan. He is both the hero and the rescuer of our lives and our minds. With a simple whisper, He revealed great weighty truths that cast out the shadows of darkness and fear. And in that instant, I recognized I was standing on the holy ground of *whatever is honorable.*

## Being careful of how we listen

As we make our way through life, we hear many voices calling out to us. The things that speak the loudest come from the world and its ideas of success or failure. They are big sounds with lots of hype and fanfare. But remember, God is often heard in the small whisper. Therefore, inclining our spiritual ears needs to be an intentional act, one that we do with purpose. How we listen is so important. God is delighted to reveal divine secrets to those who listen intently. Scripture points out that to the degree that we incline our ears, we will hear:

> For nothing is hidden that will not become evident, nor anything secret that will not be known or come to light. So take care how you listen; for whoever has more shall be given; and whoever does not have, even what he thinks he has shall be taken away from him. (Luke 8:17, 18)

Mark 4:24 puts it this way: "By your standard of measure it shall be measured to you." In other words, to the degree we incline our ears, we will be able to hear. God has a never-ending bounty of hidden counsel that He wants to reveal to us because we are His children. This vast treasure trove of wisdom and knowledge is the same type of hiddenness we talked about in the account of Esther, a bigger plan for our lives that is unstoppable. God is pleased to reveal the unseen in-workings of His kingdom.

God wants to speak to us throughout our day, and He is always within earshot. We simply need to take care to listen intently and with purpose, just as Hannah did when she approached God directly. We are encouraged in scripture to approach the throne of grace with boldness. It is a humble but diligent posture of mindfulness.

We must also be mindful that how we listen is different from what we listen to. *How* implies a skill on our part that can be cultivated; meditation hones such a skill. How we listen will influence what we listen to. When we listen in reverence, the superficial notes of life turn sharp in our ears and are no longer alluring. Instead, the melodic sounds of truth fall gently on our souls like the fresh morning dew.

During His earthly ministry, Jesus issued this statement about listening: "Whoever has ears, let them hear!" (Matthew 13:9). In this proclamation, Jesus is telling us that the words He speaks to our hearts carry great weight. That's why the statement is emphatic. God has given us spiritual ears to hear divine truths. But the second half of this verse indicates that we have the options of using or not using our spiritual ears. Although He directs us to use them, whether we use them is up to us. Using them wisely will usher in the hidden truths that God wants to unveil to our minds.

Listening with both ears is important to *how* we listen. The intricate design of the inner ear gives us interesting insight into this truth. When working properly, both ears send signals to the brain at the same time, which allows us to keep our balance. When one ear does not work as it should, it conflicts with the signal sent from the other ear and carries a false message to the brain. The person struggling with an inner ear problem, for instance, stumbles instead of walking with sure-footed certainty. So it is when we listen to God with one ear and the world with the other. It tricks our minds and causes us to perceive things in ways that makes us stumble. This is crucial insight to the importance of how we listen—and with both ears.

Jesus encourages us to get in a quiet place and close the door to pray in secret (Matthew 6). That word *secret* also means "hidden." God wants to communicate with the hidden person who finds his or her true self in Him, the private person no one else can see. He desires our full attention (both ears) as we apply ourselves to the direct access of His presence. He wants us to hear His heart in a very intentional connection. It doesn't have to be a specific room, although it can be, but rather a place where we can close the door to the world's static and noise. It may be in the backyard or on a walk. It could be sitting very still or running a lap. It could be floating in a pool or driving a car. It may be sitting behind a desk or doing laundry. But wherever it is, the door to interference must be purposely shut.

Imagine if someone asked us if she could tell us something very important. How we listen will manifest itself immediately. If we don't bother to close the door for privacy, and we look at our watches and shift about in our chairs, we will hear a limited amount of the other person's heart. But if we invite her in and close the door, sit down, look her in the eye, and listen with intent, we will hear the depths of her heart.

We all know how valuable being heard is. We have all had those times in our lives when people important to us have not listened to what we've had to say. Or perhaps they listened, but they did not hear our hearts, or at least not what was really deep inside us. They may have been busy, distracted, jaded— whatever the case, even though they had ears on their heads, they chose not to listen with full and focused intent.

Indulge me for a moment as I drive home this point even further. Imagine a child trying to communicate with an uninterested parent sitting in front of a TV day after day. Now, imagine if that same child one day decided to click off the TV, stand in front of it, face the parent, and say, "Whoever has ears, let him hear." Can you imagine the parent's shock?

How we listen to people is important, because when we do so with purposeful intent, they feel safe enough to reveal the hidden things in their heart.

What about you? You have had times where you felt as if your voice was not worth listening to. Perhaps you were met with a silence that was loud with disinterest. Or maybe someone else's preconceived ideas misinterpreted your communication. It feels bad to think someone doesn't care what you really have to say, and your words fall flat. Great pain accompanies this kind of struggle. But with God, it is different; He desires to listen to our hearts. With Him, we have a great opportunity to lay it all out and leave nothing hidden. Everything and anything on our minds is of interest to God. He wants us to share the depths of our thoughts with Him. He is the best listener.

Figuratively speaking, He closes the door, sits us down, and looks us straight in the eyes. And then He listens.

Hannah got this. She knew God would truly listen to her heart. In fact, Hannah became so focused she didn't even notice she was being observed by Eli the priest. The Lord was pleased with Hannah's earnest determination in her begging and in inclining her ear to listen. Her meditations were sweet and sacred, both speaking and listening. Meditation allows us to connect on a whole-new level. We can see this in Hannah's story.

The art of listening and meditation is not just for some; it is for all who have been given spiritual ears. It's a part our kingdom privileges. God grants us ears to hear and eyes to see. Like Hannah, we can push the limits toward accessing God directly in counsel, prayer, and meditation. He loves to be our closest confidant. There is a sacred adventure of the mind awaiting those who seek to dwell at the well of God's truth. Meditation is the best way to muse, study, commune with, and ponder the nature of God. Why would we not desire to listen in this way? The Good Shepherd delights to lead us into His kingdom realities to bring refreshment, blue skies, and wonder to the depths of our hearts, souls, and minds.

*Questions to Ponder:*

1. What self-defeating thought seems to plague you and play like a reel over and over again in your mind?
2. What happens to this destructive thinking (in the secular thought bubble) when placed before God (in the spiritual thought bubble)?
3. Intentionally listening to God requires dialing down the noise in our lives. Is there a place or time where you find this works best for you?

CHAPTER 4

# *Whatever Is Just*
## *Part One*

⟶ ✍ ⟵

I——N LIFE'S JOURNEY, NO MATTER where we travel, one thing is certain: there will be suffering. But have you ever wondered why some people don't experience as much brokenness as others? Maybe you feel that you have had more than your share. In your mind, there doesn't seem to be any good reason for the trials you've faced. But who is able to determine the value in those things that seem unjust?

My oldest daughter, Kristin, is grown up now with children of her own. But one day when she was small, she looked me straight in the eyes and announced she wanted to become a Supreme Court justice. I thought it was an unusual pursuit for a child, but I had noticed her uncanny ability to fairly assess the inherent value in complicated situations. I marveled at this coming from such a small person; after all, it takes discernment to keenly ascertain justice from a finite mind, let alone a child's mind.

But, truth be told, it is not humanly possible to assess the value of the difficulties we endure, no matter how wise we are. Even if the most brilliant minds of the world designed a computer program—one in which we could put any situation into a value meter to deliver the best-possible analysis—it would still be deficient and unable to determine the inherent value of suffering because it would be based on flawed, human calculations rather than those of the Divine Creator.

For instance, think about the people who are unimpressive on the outside but possess hidden talent. Perhaps they are at a great disadvantage because they're overlooked most of their lives, then finally the giftedness within is recognized and brought to light. Yet to a certain extent, this happens only because of the difficulties they've overcome, which have actually helped shape this gift within. We see this in movies all the time. The underdog—the one nobody thinks will make it—triumphs in the end. Although we rejoice to see the outcome of these stories, it's harder to live them. But it is in these very hardships that hidden value often surfaces.

Once again, we are met with the word *hidden*. In chapter 1, we plunged into the hidden weight that we are instructed to think about. In chapter 2, we talked about a mysterious hiddenness seen in the bigger picture, as in the story of Esther. In chapter 3, we touched on how God delights to reveal divine hidden secrets to those who listen intently. It becomes increasingly clear that the word *hidden* takes on great significance in the life of a Christian. In fact, if we dare to wrap our minds around what this might mean in our own lives personally, we will find ourselves embarking on the most marvelous of biblical mysteries. That is, God, by His masterful design, is pleased to reveal His glory in the way of hiddenness—hidden value in the unexpected, the not so typical, and the very difficult. This shouldn't surprise us because the scriptures speak so clearly of God's countercultural ways:

> God has chosen the foolish things of the world to shame the wise, and God has chosen the weak things of the world to shame the things which are strong, and the base things of the world and the despised God has chosen, the things that are not, so that He may nullify the things that are. (1 Corinthians 1:27, 28)

The better we understand this truth, the greater our ability will be to journey on the rocky roads of life that seem senseless and unjust. Remember, these verses are not random sentiments placed in the Bible to make us feel better. On the contrary, they show us deep insight into the very design of God. They cast a light on the continuous golden thread throughout scripture that leads to the most valuable yet overlooked treasure that ever was—Jesus. He is the cornerstone the builders rejected: "Have you never read in the Scriptures: 'The stone the builders rejected has become the cornerstone; the Lord has done this, and it is marvelous in our eyes'?" (Matthew 21:42).

What we can rightly conclude, then, is this: when it comes to spiritual value, we will find the most significant good is often hidden in what the world views as insignificant.

The unique story line of the Bible—that things appear inconsequential when they are not—is undeniable. Yet we might need to challenge ourselves a step further and investigate circumstances that seem plainly unfair or unjust. Surely, in situations or circumstances that are blatantly evil, we can rightly determine value. What about those senseless happenings that cause so much difficulty and pain? Yet even here we are unable to see into the deeper purposes of the divine because God alone is the ultimate justifier. He determines His plans for our individual paths, and He is fully able to use the injustices that others do to us in far-reaching ways we may never see in this lifetime.

This brings us to our fourth focus phrase from Philippians 4:8: *whatever is just*. We may not understand the greater picture of what God has done (or is doing) in our lives. Our hearts may be broken from circumstances that have befallen us. Still, we can place our surest trust in the one who will bring about whatever is just in our lives as He works on our behalf.

This is not to say that we don't fight injustice and do our part in helping ourselves and others who have been violated. We are not speaking of those necessary acts that the scripture encourages us to do, such as feeding the poor and defending the helpless. We can trust that God will make all things right in life's atrocities and bring divine retribution in the end; He will right all wrongs. Scripture states that God's wrath is being stored up to be poured out for the injustices of this world. "Vengeance is mine, I will repay, says the Lord." (Romans 12:9) It's a fearful thing to fall into the hands of the living God. Only those covered by His grace will be safe in that day.

Nevertheless, we still have to walk difficult roads that seem so unfair. The death of loved ones, disease, betrayal, divorce, brokenness, poverty—the list of human suffering is endless. We can be certain that no matter what we experience, even if it seems wildly unjust, God has a greater purpose that weaves perfectly into His eternal story, and we will someday see the glory of it.

Cultivating faith during personal seasons of crisis, darkness, and injustice is not an easy task, though, because it defies logic and reason. Faith lays itself open to the speculations and jeers from the outside world, a path that many people deem we are due. They look on in pity or insinuate we must have done something to deserve our suffering. They exercise human wisdom instead of heavenly perspective. They are usually the ones to say things that make our burden heavier to bear, like the counsel of Job's friends. We almost believe them until we catch a glimpse of God's marvelous paradigm—the hiding of great value from those who think themselves wise in their own eyes.

Consider the words of Jesus:

I praise You, Father, Lord of heaven and earth, that You have [hidden] these things from the wise and intelligent and have revealed them to infants. Yes, Father, for this way was well pleasing in Your sight. (Matthew 11:25, 26)

Notice how Jesus is conversing with His Father about these counterintuitive truths, even affirming that to unfold spiritual secrets to the humble of heart and conceal them from the haughty of mind is well pleasing in God's sight. Children are frequently the recipients of divine insights into His kingdom purposes, and He addresses the childlike heart when he says, "Do not be afraid, little flock, for your Father has been pleased to give you the kingdom" (Luke 12:32).

This is where the sacred journey of our minds takes deep root. We have talked about divine weight, have delved into the richness of whatever is true, and have been wowed by the wonder of whatever is honorable. Now we are being led into the mind-gripping reality of whatever is just. It is the ultimate laying down at the feet of the cross those things we simply do not understand. This will take some serious trust, and only the humble of heart will be able to tread the depths of its hidden value. No wonder our journey has led us first through the lovely meditating fields of weight and wonder. Truth and reverence are the catalyst for cultivating a childlike faith in the *whatever is just* of our lives, those plans and workings of God that are painful, baffling, and seemingly of no apparent value.

## Childlike faith brings hope

Our adult minds naturally want to put what seems unjust in our lives through a human value-meter—and we do. Out comes our own estimations, and they are often bitterly hopeless. We can't make sense in our minds of what has happened to us (or is happening). It seems like an unsolvable puzzle; the concept of good coming from the unimaginably bad does not compute. We may be able to wrap our minds around it theologically, but practically it fails the proof test. For this reason, God speaks to our hearts through the lives of many who have gone before us, reminding us that it is safe to trust Him no matter how outlandish our situation might seem.

Ruth in the Old Testament is one of those people. She is part of our spiritual heritage and represents the childlike faith that entrusts itself to God's plans regardless of the bleak future we seem destined to. Her mother-in-law, Naomi, on the other hand, represents the natural adult-like bitterness that comes from disillusionment and happens when life doesn't make sense.

Consider the scene. Naomi's husband had moved her two sons away from their home country to the foreign region of Moab during a famine. All seemed well when suddenly not only did her husband take ill and die, but so did both of her sons. As she began the journey of heading back to her own country with her two newly widowed daughters-in-law, she was struck with a bitter flurry of thoughts. Somewhere between the start of their journey and this point, she put all her circumstances through the value-meter of her human, finite mind. What came out was a collage of remorse, regret, and an ultimate giving in to her perceived hopeless situation. She wrongly ascribed value in finding happiness and a future for her daughters-in-law in returning home. Consequently, she also wrongly conveyed the lack of value in continuing the journey with her.

What's interesting to note is that although her pleadings were misguided, they made great sense. Naomi said,

> Return home, my daughters. Why would you come with me? Am I going to have any more sons, who could become your husbands? Return home, my daughters; I am too old to have another husband. Even if I thought there was still hope for me—even if I had a husband tonight and then gave birth to sons—would you wait until they grew up? Would you remain unmarried for them? No, my daughters. It is more bitter for me than for you, because the Lord's hand has turned against me! (Ruth 1:11–13)

By all sound reason, these words seemed wise, sacrificial, and filled with good intention. And coming from a matriarchal figure added even more weight. This is a good reminder that logical reasoning doesn't automatically indicate we are making the right decisions or going in the best direction.

Ruth, on the other hand, was determined to commit herself to God's plan even when it didn't make sense. Her response to her mother-in-law defied reason and logic: "Where you go I will go, and where you stay I will stay. Your people will be my people, and your God my God" (Ruth 1:16). Ruth exhibited a kind of faith that was childlike. She was placing her trust in a plan that held the unknown, one the average person could punch plenty of holes in— and Naomi did. Yet Ruth dug her heels in regardless of the bleak, hopeless future Naomi painted that accompanied such a choice. Ultimately, Ruth was willing to be led by God into whatever He saw fit and whatever He thought right for her life. Disregarding the outcome, she placed her faith in God.

We can also note that although these two women were experiencing similar life circumstances, they were processing them differently. Observe the opposing weights between Naomi's hopelessness and Ruth's willingness to trust God during a season of injustice. Ruth had resolved to follow God into the unknown, whereas Naomi came up with her own faulty plan. Also, Ruth's willingness to be away from the comfort of what was familiar contrasted to Naomi's seeking the familiar as a means of comfort.

Naomi's disheartenment is obvious in her request to be called by a new name that meant "bitter." She said, "Do not call me Naomi; call me Mara, for the Almighty has dealt very bitterly with me" (Ruth 1:20). Naomi's feelings are normal to the human experience. Most people can attest to feeling hopeless at one point or another in their lives. Sometimes, it comes on all of a sudden; oftentimes, it builds over years. Hopelessness is a state of having no expectation or hope for success. People who find themselves in a hopeless frame of mind feel at a complete loss. The dark clouds shroud their minds to the point of doubting blue skies even exist. They simply lose confidence, and depression sets in.

We should not be surprised to struggle with these types of feelings. Not only is this normal, but many seasoned saints have systematically battled with dark nights of the soul pleading for hope. Martin Luther reeled on the ground in agonizing prayer in a desperate season. Charles Spurgeon struggled with stomach ailments due to his spiritual discouragement. Hudson Taylor, the great missionary to China, had an emotional breakdown, and the list goes on.

We will never be able to get away from the fact that even though we are Christians, we are still human. The Lord did not throw in the towel concerning Naomi simply because she was bitter or feeling hopeless. On the contrary, what we see here in this story is a beautiful picture of God's rescuing grace as He brings Ruth across Naomi's path. Ruth's determination served as a great weight of light in a very dark season of Naomi's life. Ruth was an unlikely vessel, yet her actions were a tall drink of water in a parched, barren desert. Like the rock in the wilderness that poured forth waters to the disillusioned and wandering Israelites, God provided hope for Naomi through Ruth. Faith is the ultimate watering can, and it was God's provision to hydrate Naomi's path through Ruth.

What wonderful hidden good we find here. The weight of hope that Ruth's faith exhibited caused the blue skies to break through Naomi's dark clouds of despair. It is interesting that Ruth didn't offer solutions. She didn't sugarcoat the circumstances to Naomi or offer pep talks. Ruth truly did not know what it would mean to follow God; she simply embarked into the uncharted waters of whatever God deemed just in a great season of injustice.

We see many accounts of faith in the face of injustice in the Bible. For instance, when David was pelted by stones and verbally harassed, he did not rise up in defense or allow his officials to strike down the accusers. He left justice in God's hands, saying, "If he is cursing because the Lord said to him, 'Curse David,' who can ask, 'Why do you do this?' Let him alone" (2 Samuel 16:10–12).

Shadrach, Meshach, and Abednego trusted God despite the fiery fate awaiting them. Meshach responded,

> King Nebuchadnezzar, we do not need to defend ourselves before you in this matter. If we are thrown into the blazing furnace, the God we serve is able to deliver us from it, and he will deliver us from Your Majesty's hand. But even if he does not, we want you to know, Your Majesty, that we will not serve your gods or worship the image of gold you have set up. (Daniel 3:17, 18)

Take special note of the phrases *the God we serve is able* and *but even if he does not*. In essence, these young men were making a conscious decision to trust in what they knew to be true concerning God—rather than the circumstances or the outcome of the trial. They put their faith in God's choice for their lives. The words they spoke were packed with spiritual weight illuminating that God was able to do all things with great and equal ease. One thing is not harder than another for God to accomplish. Parting the Red Sea is just as easy as healing the blind. Raising a person from the dead is just as easy as giving another stamina. With this said, we can rightly ascertain that if God chooses to allow things that don't seem right, we can trust that it is a part of a sovereign plan that He alone holds the design to.

Remember, a vast blue sky remains in place even if God chooses to keep it hidden for a season by a layer of clouds. As soon as John the Baptist baptized Jesus in the Jordan River, he witnessed God's divine ability when the sky opened up and a voice said, "This is my beloved son," speaking of Jesus. Yet it closed up during the dark season of doubt when John questioned whether

Christ was really the Messiah. Jesus sent a message to encourage John that the kingdom was, indeed, coming alive all around him: "Go and tell John what you have seen and heard: the blind receive their sight, the lame walk, lepers are cleansed, and the deaf hear, the dead are raised up, the poor have good news preached to them" (Luke 7:22).

But what Jesus spoke next is crucial and should not escape our notice, especially in a season of injustice: "Blessed is anyone who does not stumble on account of me" (Matthew 11:16). In other words, when life seems unfair, it's easy to stumble, especially when we think God could do something about it but chooses not to. John's predicament was certainly not what he expected. His personal dilemma was going from bad to worse. Jesus did not deny his difficultly but offered hope by helping John look outside the darkness of his circumstances to the soul revolution that he was a coparticipant in God's eternal plan of salvation through Jesus Christ, even while in prison. There was something bigger happening that John would be a part of forever.

Of course, the most natural response when something seems unjust is to ask, "Why is God allowing this?" We all have the human tendency to determine, based on our circumstances, that God is unjust, even if we do it unconsciously. Or, we reason that God has somehow overlooked us or doesn't value us as much as others. So, when things start going wrong, we naturally doubt. We wrestle and writhe in pain at the inability to find value in the difficult road we are being forced to walk. Our minds calculate and recalculate without results until we are wearied. It's not until we finally come to the end of our deductions and surrender our judgments that we find the Ruth-like place of the heart that simply says, "I will take this road God is leading me on in faith regardless of the outcome."

*Questions to Ponder:*

1. Have people offered the burden of human wisdom that made a situation in your life even more difficult to endure? How did that affect you?

2.  Can you recall a season where you felt as if you were in a foreign land or where it felt as if you were under a layer of darkness with no hope of blue skies breaking through?

3.  Can you identify with Naomi being refreshed by Ruth's faith? Has someone or some event represented hope and refreshment to your heart?

# Whatever Is Just
## Part Two

⎯⎯⎯⎯ ৩ ⎯⎯⎯⎯

WE MIGHT BE SURPRISED BY what is one of the greatest obstacles to successfully traveling a difficult road. It's not the difficulty; it's us, the travelers. We are the ones who get in the way of what God is doing. Like Naomi, when she tried to send Ruth back to Moab, we block the path for ourselves and for others. If we were able to grasp the consequences of our faulty fix-it plans, we would drop them immediately. For Ruth, a blocked path would have meant giving up a future that held a loving husband, children, and eternal blessings. For Naomi, it would have been giving up the grandchild who would be part of the lineage of the Messiah. The bottom line is that the only way to get out of our own way is to mentally let go of the plans that have changed.

Letting go of the ideas of what we thought life should be like is not easy. It requires yielding to something that feels very strange to us. Life-altering events like death, divorce, betrayal, violation, sickness, job loss, and natural disasters are traumatic. It's hard to endorse something that is against our aspirations for the future. There's death involved—death to a dream, an ideal. To embrace it would mean to let go and pick up the new unknown plan—like a cross—and follow God in a different direction from what we may have anticipated. It takes a great deal of flexibility and dependence not only to lay down a dream but to pick up a different one that may bring anguish to the heart.

Childlike faith is necessary to journey through these times in our lives. To successfully navigate requires baby steps. We are misdirected if we think heroic, adult-like strength gets us through; this mind-set is sure to fail. The truth is that it takes childlike faith in the One who is able, regardless of what happens. It can be tricky because we have to be sensitive to God's leading in order to follow. Assumptions do not do well here. Rushing doesn't work. Pressure makes it worse. Coleading is a flop. There is no other way but the hard work of baby steps, one foot at a time with an outstretched hand that reaches into the hand of a mighty God. Like the broken heart that becomes aware of its next breath, this kind of faith hangs on to God tightly to survive.

This means letting go of every other impulse. Some would say it's giving up, but when God is leading, it's OK to quietly relinquish control. It is yielding with hope like Ruth rather than in defeat, as in Naomi's case.

Christ gave us a good picture of what that looks like when He was led by his Father's will down the road to Golgotha: "He was led like a lamb to the slaughter, and as a sheep before its shearers is silent, so he did not open his mouth" (Isaiah 53:7). God could be trusted to walk His Son through this immense road of injustice. It was a plan set before the hand of time; it was not thrown together and randomly accomplished. It was the turning point of history, the climax of all things eternal. Because of hindsight, we know that the greater plan was wrought through injustice and that a just and perfect man would die in place of all the unjust, thereby securing justice for all.

Christians often hold to the mistaken mind-set that once they become believers, their path will be more prosperous, less difficult. It's true that the soul prospers in an abundance of spiritual refreshment that gets us through the trials of life. In fact, we are delving into those kingdom benefits in this book. But at the same time, the devil is more intent to deliberately plant the weeds of chaos in the gardens of our hearts. Consider this scripture, and notice his method:

The kingdom of God is like a man who sowed good seed in his field. But while everyone was sleeping, his enemy came and sowed weeds among the wheat, and went away. When the wheat sprouted and formed heads, the weeds also appeared. The owner's servants came to him and said, "Sir, didn't you sow good seed in your field? Where then did the weeds come from?"

"An enemy did this," he replied.

"Do you want us to go and pull them up?"

"No," he answered. "Because while you are pulling the weeds, you may uproot the wheat with them. Let them both grow together until harvest. At that time I will tell the harvesters: First collect the weeds and tie them in bundles to be burned; then gather the wheat and bring it into my barn." (Matthew 13:24–30)

This parable makes it clear that we will live our journeys with evil present. If I base my security in Christ on a perfect garden with no weeds, I will be constantly discouraged. This is because we live in a fallen world where good and evil exist together. In my early days of faith, I was rocked every time bad things happened to me. I felt compelled to be on a constant weed-pulling mission. I spent all my days fruitlessly obsessing over trying to create a weed-less path rather than trusting the weeds to the harvester. Once I understood that weeds—the evil the devil sows—were an inevitable part of life, I focused on planting and watering instead of just pulling. Yes, a healthy garden needs tending, and that includes pulling weeds, but there is so much more to a beautiful garden. Because we live in a broken world that has not been fully redeemed, we will journey with pebbles in our shoes, thorns in our sides, and weeds in our gardens.

## God's hidden good is unstoppable

If we are finally grasping the theme of all things and circumstances, good and bad, coming together for one great story—God's story—then we are getting it! But how can we say that which is bad is good? It's important to note that we are not talking about calling evil good. We are acknowledging that God can make good the difficult path we have been called to walk, even a path where evil has trodden. In Ruth and Naomi's case, a greater good lay on the other side of awful. This goodness is accomplished through Christ—it's the good news of rescue! For instance, when "Good" Friday came, it was a horrific day for Christ to endure at the hands of evil. Yet it is called good not because it was easy or in any way aesthetically pleasing but because of the goodness that would be poured out on many souls because Jesus journeyed such an unthinkable and unjust road.

Even our bad and regretful choices will be used for His glory as in Joseph's life when his brothers plotted his demise. Many years later, when they trembled in his presence with great fear for the deeds they committed, Joseph, seeing their great anxiety, comforted them with these words, revealing hidden value: "You intended to harm me, but God intended it for good to accomplish what is now being done, the saving of many lives" (Genesis 50:20). Again we see good rising from the bad.

When considering good in this way, it isn't a good that's humanly calculable or visible. It is spiritual with incalculable significance. This kind of good has hidden value that can be assessed only by God because He has designed or allowed it. It's a promise, part of our kingdom benefits: "And we know that God causes all things to work together for good to those who love God, to those who are called according to His purpose" (Romans 8:28).

Difficult situations can look hopeless in our lives and appear to have no purpose—like barren soil with no apparent sign of life. Yet after being tilled and fertilized, the soil becomes the backdrop of something glorious and full of majestic brilliance, a garden that bursts forth with new growth. It does not stay broken and plowed. Remember, we have a great farmer with marvelous plans for His garden: "Does the farmer plow continually to plant seed? Does he continually turn and harrow the ground?" (Isaiah 28:24). No, eventually, good springs forth.

Ruth's life displayed this kind of hope during a very difficult journey. But her sister-in-law, Orpah, who was on the exact same journey, was swept away by the weight of cynicism that her mother-in-law presented. The influence was remarkable because Orpah's entire destiny was affected by the weeds of Naomi's negative spirit. A cynical heart is the opposite of childlike faith. It is full of distrust, and like a heavy weight, it keeps the mind bogged down. Cynicism digs not only its own grave but the graves of others. It darkens the ability to see and interferes with the ability to hear. The funny thing is, the more mature with age we get in this life, the more we tend to become cynical. Skeptical views develop from being let down over time. Life has a way of doing this in a progressive manner. That's why to cultivate a childlike faith requires a type of "retrogression" from the naturally growing cynical spirit inside of all of us. This explains why older Christians seem to lose fervor.

But why should we trust our jaded perspective with the navigation of our life? That's just not safe! More than at any other time in our lives, when we're in a season of injustice, we must cultivate trust in God rather than ourselves. As A. W. Tozer puts it in his book *The Pursuit of God*, "We are often hindered from giving up our treasures to the Lord out of fear for their safety...yet everything is safe which we commit to Him, and nothing is really safe which is not so committed."

If bitterness has been an issue for you, take great comfort in God's tender grace toward Naomi. Bitterness naturally makes it harder to find answers in life, but it's OK not to have all the answers. Comfort can be found in laying down your swords of justice and reason at the feet of the One who knows all the details of your hardship. Bring this truth out of God's treasure box and bind it to your heart: "We do not know what to do, but our eyes are on you" (2 Chronicles 20:12). Childlike faith is the safest place for the heart to dwell.

The simple truth is that faith has no agenda; it merely trusts like a child who intertwines his fingers into his parents' hands and waits for them to take the lead. We must do the same and wait on the Lord, not in inactivity but in a faith that presses on while at the same time is quiet in the spirit—no whining, stomping, or grumbling. Waiting in the original Hebrew of the Old Testament means to twist strands together like a rope, or to bind. Our primary task during difficult times is to bind ourselves to the Lord, to become so entwined and united with Him that whatever the outcome, we are secure in His unmovable love and sure of His good in our lives and in the lives of others, taking baby steps all the way. Remember, each one of us is a story within a bigger story—God's story. And in God's story, He always brings about justice where injustice has entered.

As I look back and consider my daughter's desire to become a Supreme Court justice, I am no longer surprised. In fact, it makes perfect sense when considering God's marvelous paradigm of revealing wisdom to His little flock—children—and those with childlike faith. True value comes naturally to children. They are uninhibited with the negativity and cynicism that plague the adult mind, and they are quick to forgive.

As God tends the garden of our minds, we must remember that becoming a child is part of the intended cultivation process. This small jewel of grand proportions is hidden, just waiting for us to take hold of it. Trusting God like a babe under looming clouds of darkness will eventually yield some of the bluest skies we have ever seen. May we in childlike faith trust the Lord in the *whatever is just* times of our lives.

*Questions to Ponder:*

1.  Have you had to let go of some dreams of what you thought your life would be like?
2.  Are there areas of your life where you feel as if you are on a constant weed-pulling mission?
3.  Can you see where more childlike faith is needed on your journey?

CHAPTER 5

# Whatever Is Pure
# Part One

IMAGINE YOU ARE WALKING TOWARD a pristine clearing in the Amazon rainforest. There is a beautiful spot for meditation at the water's edge that you visited the day before. As you wind your way toward it, you eventually lose sight of it through the trees, and you find yourself on a path thick with dense foliage. You push through a tangle of vines only to be blocked again by another, and another. A wave of emotions sweeps over you—fear, anxiety, and a feeling that you might not find your way out. You are utterly lost.

This analogy is much like the tangle of emotions we struggle with as we wind our way through this life, oftentimes without any true idea of where they might lead us. Although emotions are a necessary part of functioning, they can be a force to be reckoned with when inflated, manipulated, or misplaced. Hacking our way through a confusing maze of disappointment, dismay, hurt, etc., we wonder if we're ever going to find our way out.

Let me give you an example of how easily emotions can take us off track. One night when my kids were young and it was late in the evening, we heard a large crashing sound on the other side of the house. It sounded like someone breaking in, possibly a home invasion, so we wasted no time dialing 911. The police accidentally arrived at our neighbor's house two doors down, looked through the window, and saw a black man with his arms around a white woman. With the heightened emotions that come with racial profiling, they banged on the door with guns drawn, thinking there was a crime in progress. What they didn't realize was they were at the wrong house, the house of a lovely married couple who happened to be personal friends of ours and who belonged to our local church.

Our friends were simply enjoying a movie night together when the cops started beating on their door. The husband—who, coincidentally, was a policeman in the next county over—opened the door and tried to reason with the local officers. But they had already been persuaded by emotion to take him down. They shouted for him to drop to the ground, and even as my friend pleaded with them to check his credentials, they would not be swayed until he was down on his knees with his hands behind his head. It was an awful and humiliating experience. My friend dealt with it graciously and with class, but my husband and I were astounded by the intensity of exaggerated emotion that drove this scene.

Meanwhile, we soon discovered that the noise was simply a shelf in our garage that came crashing down that evening. All this drama for two families was based on nothing—just emotion.

We are all victims of inflated emotions at one point or another. Our emotions can drive us to do or think things that we ordinarily might not. It's alarming to consider that unseen forces are constantly trying to sabotage our feelings. Like a scene out of the movie *The Wizard of Oz*, our emotions are easily manipulated. Dorothy is terrified of the wizard, who is only a frail man behind a curtain projecting a blown-up image of himself. The devil does the same, provoking us by pushing just the right emotional buttons, magnifying his influence to inflated levels. This causes all kinds of wrong perceptions and miscommunication, and miscommunication is his specialty. When our minds operate from this space, our thinking goes from reasonable to irrational in a matter of seconds, and we make flawed choices based on our distorted feelings.

## Examples of emotional takeover in the Bible

It isn't hard to find examples in scripture where a takeover of emotions can be observed. For instance, while Christ was in the garden of Gethsemane praying before His crucifixion, He asked His disciples to pray with Him, but they fell asleep instead. Let's read what the scripture says:

> Jesus went out as usual to the Mount of Olives, and his disciples followed him. On reaching the place, he said to them, "Pray that you will not fall into temptation." He withdrew about a stone's throw beyond them, knelt down and prayed, "Father, if you are willing, take this cup from me; yet not my will, but yours be done." An angel from heaven appeared to him and strengthened him. And being in anguish, he prayed more earnestly, and his sweat was like drops of blood falling to the ground. When he rose from prayer and went back to the disciples, he found them asleep. (Luke 22:29–46)

We can't help but be moved by Christ's display of emotions in this narrative, which is a good reminder that it's not wrong to have emotion; it's part of being human. But for the sake of our subject, I want us to consider the disciples' emotions. What was going on inside of them that they fell asleep even after Christ asked them to stay awake and pray with Him? How could they possibly nap in such perilous times? Our first thought might be that they were being lazy, but this was not the case. Verse 46 gives good insight into the hijacking of emotions that can take place inside any of us: "When he rose from prayer and went back to the disciples, he found them asleep, exhausted from sorrow."

There it is: sorrow. Sorrow had overtaken them, and they could not stay awake. Laziness had nothing to do with it. An emotional overthrow of anguish had subverted their ability to remain awake and alert and to pray. In other words, their emotions carried them into sleep as a way of escape.

Heightened emotions can overtake any of us in many ways. They can make us tired, angry, frightened, saddened, sick, confused, and burdened, to name a few. This can be likened to a tide pool. When ocean waves wash over rocks and recede, small pools form. The living organisms that are meant to live freely in the vast sea become limited to their new environment. We, too, get stuck in tide pools of unhealthy emotion. Let me mention a few to see if they resonate with you.

Have you ever found yourself so desperate to be understood that you over-shared your feelings? And because there was little response on the other end, you reshared, reforming your words again to communicate one more time. You are floundering in the emotional tide pool of overcommunicating.

Perhaps you waste inordinate amounts of productive time worrying about things over which you have no control, thus allowing your life to be consumed by worry instead of productive activity. Or maybe you struggle with appre-hension about your abilities. Do you become easily immobilized in social set-tings and miss out on great opportunities in life?

Maybe you wrestle with insecurity, which makes you hyperspeculative, imagining things that are not necessarily true. For instance, you might have thought someone snubbed you when it seemed as if they ignored you, but really they didn't see you walk by. Or you might feel rejected and forgotten when someone doesn't reach out to you after what seems like a long time, when really they're consumed with their own daily struggles of work, worry, and keeping up with the demands of their family.

Perhaps you spend all your time trying to manage others' emotions. You are OK as long as those whom you're connected to are OK with you. But in this broken mind-set, you are too busy fixing people's views of you to enjoy living your own life. When someone is not OK with you, you lose your iden-tity to a certain extent because you have based it on who you are in their eyes.

Another area of struggle is discouragement. This one can be very emotionally crippling because it shuts down your capabilities. If you are criticized while working on an important project, discouragement creeps into your spirit and dampens your efforts. As the years pass by, you might experience a deep sense of regret (another emotion) because you have not completed your meaningful contribution to the world or fulfilled your purpose in life.

There is also bitterness, which can cause the kind of breakdown where you lose a relationship completely. You can't get past the hurt or wound, so you give up contact. Or perhaps you remain in touch, but you're never as close as you once were because you relive the pain that person caused you over and over again.

Then there are the little white lies we tell ourselves, prompted by emotions. It starts off with a small fib, and the next thing we know we are in a web of manipulation of our own creation as we try to keep up with what we've told ourselves and others. Such was the case with Rebekah in the Old Testament.

## *Rebekah's emotions*

Rebekah's story starts off sweetly. After Abraham prayed for a wife for his beloved, son Isaac, he sent out his trusted servant to search for just the right woman. The servant returned with beautiful young Rebekah. If you remember the story, Isaac had been meditating in the field when he looked up and saw a caravan of camels approaching with his lovely bride-to-be. You can almost envision the scene as Rebekah dismounts her camel, covers her face with a veil, and walks with tentative and then eager steps toward the strong and handsome Isaac. The words in scripture *Isaac loved her* give a happily-ever-after feel. But even the best stories can go off track with emotional hijacking.

What happened to this ideal union? How did it go from the hand of God bringing these two people together in sheer happiness to absolute heartbreak? As with Rebekah, many times an emotion we are feeling is so strong that it absorbs our attention. Because inflated emotions can be inwardly loud, they have a way of doing this effectively.

Rebekah and Isaac were married twenty years before having children. Eventually, Rebekah became pregnant. But much to her dismay, the pregnancy was turbulent. There were no ultrasounds back then to let her know she was having twins. She began experiencing upheaval inside her womb in what the Bible describes as jostling. The babies literally wrestled each other for dominance as they grew and developed inside of Rebekah. We can sense her despair when she says, "Why is this happening to me?" The Lord answered her question with this prophecy:

> Two nations are in your womb, and two peoples from within you will
> be separated; one people will be stronger than the other, and the older
> will serve the younger. (Genesis 25:23)

When I was a young woman, I found out I was having twins three months into my pregnancy. I was so excited and walked on clouds for the duration of the pregnancy. I gave birth to my two beautiful daughters, Abby and Ali, who shared a close connection growing up, even having baby girls within days of each other. My heart delighted in observing their unique twin-bond over the years. Unfortunately, this was not the positive outlook that Rebekah would enjoy. Her news was shocking. The friction and separation that would mark her sons' lives was already happening inside her womb. Plus, the older serving the younger was contrary to custom. Remember, Rebekah had already waited twenty years to conceive. As parents, we have ideals of what we want our families to be like. When time passes and things don't turn out the way we had hoped, we adjust. But Rebekah was not given the luxury of transition time; her dreams turned upside down in an instant.

When life challenges hit us by surprise and cause distress, we are catapulted into an emotional crisis. Emotions are not reasonable when this happens. Think about a time in your life when you faced an emotional crisis. Do you remember the havoc of feelings that instantly flooded your world? Perhaps you were all over the place trying to ease the pain, or possibly you shut down completely. Either way, you knew you had been instantly placed in the cauldron of emotions. Rebecca's long-awaited pregnancy instantly turned into a trial that worsened with time.

Early on, Rebekah's boys began running opposite directions with very different and distinct personalities. Sweet Jacob soon became her favorite, while rough-and-tumble Esau was more pleasing to Isaac. Here we begin to see the obvious signs of another kind of emotional overthrow within the family. Most people don't recognize favoritism as a sin driven by emotion, but it is, and it has far-reaching effects. As the boys grew, so did the separation within the family. There was no hiding the alliances. Even the boys were keenly aware. The sweet, faith-filled Rebekah we once saw giving up everything she knew to trust and follow God's plan in her young life was now desperately grasping, not trusting, and manipulating to achieve a desired outcome, all driven by emotion.

We, like Rebekah, also have broken dreams. It's part of living in a fallen world. But just because hardships wash us over jagged rocks and form emotional tide pools doesn't mean we are destined to stay there—even if we are facing a very different kind of life from what we thought. Philippians 4:8 reminds us that God has made a way for us to walk through our difficult emotions. In fact, verses 6 and 7 in this passage of scripture assure us of this: "Do not be anxious about anything, but in every situation, by prayer and petition, with thanksgiving, present your requests to God. And the peace of God, which transcends all understanding, will guard your hearts and your minds in Christ Jesus." This kind of peace is what we all need when our world is turned upside down. Our emotions will naturally take us off track, but it is God's desire to restore our hearts and mind in Him through the power of the Holy Spirit.

This brings us to our fifth focus phrase, *whatever is pure.* It is the product of centering our reasoning abilities under the washing and regenerating power of the Holy Spirit, regardless of how we feel. To receive a fresh application of God's presence is a powerful thing. This divine contact soothes our wayward emotions, churning with inflated feelings, and purifies our thoughts. This analogy can be fittingly aligned to the spiritual sense of touch. When the Spirit touches our runaway emotions, a purifying happens instantly. Our hearts and minds are suffused with structure and calmness like the raging sea that calmed the moment Jesus commanded it to be still.

We can observe this kind of power attributed to the Spirit all the way back in Genesis 1:2: "The earth was without form and void, and darkness was over the face of the deep. And the Spirit of God was hovering over the face of the waters." In the original Hebrew of the Old Testament, the words *without form* mean "chaos." God's Spirit moved over the chaos and majestically implemented order. His plan is to do the same for us in the chaos and confusion of our wayward emotions. His Spirit hovers over our hearts, moving over our minds and bringing peaceful order to our otherwise raging emotions that have trapped us on overgrown paths or in rocky, jagged tide pools.

It is the divine presence of the Holy Spirit, the unseen holding of His hand, that brings order to our otherwise chaotic pilgrimage here on Earth. A true strengthening of the heart can be accomplished only by Him, the great Comforter and promised Helper. Jesus told the disciples that He must go so that the Comforter could come: "But I tell you the truth, it is to your advantage that I go away; for if I do not go away, the Helper will not come to you; but if I go, I will send Him to you" (John 16:7). When we are overshadowed by the darkened clouds of emotion, only the touch of the Holy Spirit can part those clouds to reveal the blue skies beyond.

*Questions to Ponder:*

1.  Can you identify with any of the emotional tide pool examples in this chapter? What effects have those had on your life?
2.  Have you ever experienced a crisis where you felt placed in a cauldron of emotions?
3.  Can you recall a time in your life when your emotions were instantly soothed by a touch from the Holy Spirit?

# Whatever Is Pure
## Part Two

⟶

*I* MUST WARN YOU THAT the peace of mind that transcends understanding does not come easily. Nefarious forces fan the flames of
our emotions, keeping us far from the Holy Spirit's influence. And
feelings, when inflated, naturally turn into bullies that put pressure on our
thought-life. In fact, our own inflated emotions can be the biggest giants
we face in life. They tell us something bad is happening, and we must act.
Unfortunately, those actions usually turn out to be self-defeating.

Like Rebekah, we take matters into our hands, and the fallout of our own
destructive choices becomes evident as life comes crashing down around us.
Proverbs 14:1 highlights this dynamic: "The wise woman builds her house, but
the foolish tears it down with her own hands." We are often aghast at the destruction caused by our own heightened emotional responses. Sometimes, it even feels
as if aliens have taken over our bodies. After the fact, we wish we could go back in
time and respond differently. For Rebekah, it became very clear that her world had
fallen apart when the one son she favored was ultimately banished from her life.

## Emotions can quench the Holy Spirit

Another effect of inflated emotions is the stifling of the Holy Spirit. We are
cautioned in 1 Thessalonians 5:19: "Do not quench the Spirit." Although there

are other ways to do this, an emotional overthrow is arguably the most common. It's akin to dumping a large bucket of dirt on top of a thriving fire. In this case, the fire is that of the Holy Spirit, the small inner presence that flickers inside of us. One minute, the coals are burning; the next, they are doused. The chill of emotions takes over, and our reasoning abilities become frosty as we lose the warmth of the Spirit. Have you ever felt an icy feeling come over you that doesn't seem to care what kind of damage it causes? That's because wayward emotions are freezing out the good ones. I've been astounded at the coldness of my heart at times when I've experienced emotional detachment to healthy feelings. We've all been there.

This, in turn, grieves the Spirit (Ephesians 4:30). It's compelling to consider the magnitude of this. Even though we are mere mortals, the Holy Spirit is saddened and made sorrowful by the quenching of His influence in our lives and minds. Let's take a moment to let that truly sink in: He has His own emotions. We may not have really understood that He gets grieved in this way. He is saddened when we allow faulty or darkened thoughts to reside in our hearts. It pains Him when we don't grasp the truth He places in front of us. He wants to lead our minds into the blue skies of His heavenly thinking, but we settle for the cold fog of the lowlands. He is saddened on our behalf and for our sake, and He does not want our overwrought emotions to stifle His influence in our lives. He simply desires to touch our minds to *purify* and restore our thinking.

*Emotions can throw us off balance*

Earlier in the book, I mentioned briefly the difficulties associated with overthrowing the delicate balance of the inner ear. But taking a closer look at vertigo gives us further insight into the effects of wayward emotions. Vertigo is the sensation that the room is circling around us when it is not. During the writing of this book, I woke up one morning to a severe case of it. I couldn't get down the hall without falling. I called for my husband. He helped me to the bathroom, where I vomited violently. Next, I was rushed to the emergency room, where tests were done to make sure I wasn't having a stroke. Further testing showed that my left inner ear was abnormally functioning and was sending what my physical therapist called aberrant signals to the brain. The word *aberrant* means "deviant." It's a signal that has deviated from what is truly happening. It felt as if the room were spinning because of this one aberrant signal. The other functions of the body were sending healthy signals, but because this one ear was unhealthy, it caused confusion in all the other bodily signals.

It is amazing to think that one little aberrant signal can dominate the entire body. In the same way, during a season of difficulty, our feelings might spin wildly out of control and monopolize our minds. Our confidence flies out the window, and our reasoning abilities become faulty. The brain is saying one thing, whereas reality is saying another. As with vertigo, the only sense of relief comes from lying perfectly still. All other efforts cause dizziness and worsen the sensation of spinning.

If you have ever had a season where your emotions felt like this, you know what I am talking about. The harder you tried to keep up with your feelings, the worse things got. Sometimes, God allows our equilibriums to be shaken for a season so that we might recognize our need to let go of all self-efforts. The touch of His Spirit is our only hope over emotional ambush.

The Lord knows we are but humans, incapable of rescuing ourselves. I can't think of a better opportunity to heed God's instructions: "Be still and know that I am God" (Psalm 46:10). As with vertigo, spinning emotions do not respond well to movement. There are times when we must be very still and allow the Spirit to hover over the chaos of our spiraling emotions.

*Emotions can poison our thinking*

It doesn't end there; quenching of the Spirit opens the door to poisonous thinking. This is where our thoughts become contaminated by our emotions. How can we recognize when this is happening? The word *poison* in the dictionary means "a substance that inhibits the activity of another substance or the course of a reaction or process." In terms of the spiritual mind, this would be when emotion inhibits the activity or direction of God's purpose for our thinking. Signs of impairment include an inability to think in spiritual terms or to see God's truth clearly.

When it comes to our thoughts about the people we know, our emotions can cause a level of toxicity that poisons our minds toward them. If you have been on the receiving end of this, you know what I am talking about. No matter how hard you try, a person whose mind has been poisoned against you simply will not like you. It often feels like a losing battle, and that's exactly what Satan wants. He is trying to steal thoughts of goodwill—whether it's others' goodwill toward you or your goodwill toward others. If it is someone you care deeply about, you may experience a deep sense of loss when his or her heart is turned against you. You might even notice that it becomes contagious, passed on to others. We can see that when Rebekah's emotions became toxic. They poisoned her thinking, which in turn poisoned her sons' thinking.

*Emotions ignite impulsive reactions*

If I have convinced you of the power of emotions and the damage they can cause, then I must offer that exaggerated emotions can also fuel momentum. Some people tend to burn bridges when this happens. I always caution people who are in the middle of an emotional trial to avoid making major life choices. Waiting is a crucial counterstep to impulse. Heightened emotions can give us a false sense of bravery or desperation to do things we might not otherwise do.

Years ago when I recognized this pattern, I decided to try an experiment. When an offense occurred, instead of immediate confrontation, I wrote a letter expressing my raw feelings. I did not send the letter but folded it and set it aside until the next day. This was very cathartic in that I was able to honestly express my emotions in the moment. Working through emotions with the help of the Lord is therapeutic. The next day, I reread the letter and was shocked by some of the emotions I expressed. They were so intense. Resisting the impulse to act made a difference. One day removed naturally brought these thoughts to a more temperate level. It's interesting to consider that self-control is one of the fruits of the Spirit. It was tremendously beneficial to hold myself to a twenty-four-hour response time by writing down my feelings instead of acting on them, and it gave me an entirely different perspective.

Notice that the scripture encourages the kind of wisdom that comes with restraining our own spirit: "He who is slow to anger is better than the mighty, and he who rules his spirit, than he who captures a city" (Proverbs 16:32). Wow, that's a weighty endorsement of self-control, even placing its value above a skilled warrior. In other words, controlling our emotions is greater than the impressiveness of war heroes. Self-control guards against the destruction that can accompany an emotional invasion. Of course we don't always have the luxury of waiting, but if we do, we will find that it opens the door to a fresh and powerful infusion of the Holy Spirit concerning our emotions. I was able to take the time to pray over my conversation and allow the leading and reasoning of the Holy Spirit to help me rewrite the letter, and boy was it different.

## Common thread of influence

One thing is for certain: when it comes to the damaging effects of inflated emotions, we will always find the common thread of influence. Whether it's destruction, quenching, imbalance, impulse, or poison, we are being influenced. This influence parallels intoxication. Rogue emotions cause us to do, say, and think things we might never ordinarily dream of. As if we were inebriated, inflated emotions can cause reckless indiscretion.

Envision a bottle of emotions set on one end of a table, calling out like a strong drink. If certain emotions are a problem in our lives, then resisting their consumption will be difficult, as if we were alcoholics. But also like alcoholics, we are never fully cured; therefore, we must turn away from the drink of inflated emotions that we know will bring ruin, and turn toward the Holy Spirit.

Accountability in this area is valuable. We can imagine the setting being much like an AA meeting. How interesting that would be.

"Hello, my name is Paula, and I struggle with fear."

"Hi, Paula. Tell us a little about yourself."

"Well, I first noticed a tendency toward this emotion when I had a traumatic experience as a girl."

This might seem like a lighthearted take on the subject, but role-playing helps us grasp the seriousness of the stronghold that emotions can have over us.

*Questions to Ponder:*

1. Can you identify a time when your emotions caused destruction in your circumstances?
2. Have you ever felt emotionally detached and icy toward spiritual things or thoughts? Can you remember a time when you quenched the Holy Spirit? Have your emotions ever made you feel under the influence?
3. Emotions can poison our thoughts toward others and their thoughts toward us. Think of a time in your life when you experienced this. How did it affect you and your relationships with others?

# Whatever Is Pure
## Part Three

⟿

WHERE DO WE START? How do we begin the process of getting our emotional overthrows under control? Is it possible to break free from life's tangle of emotions? Hebrews 12:3 offers a solution: "Let us also lay aside every weight and sin which clings so closely, and let us run with endurance the race that is set before us."

The laying aside of these weights requires action on our part. This verse indicates that these weights are knowable, which means the first step requires observation. We must investigate our emotional backgrounds with the Lord's help to discover what these weights are.

If we look back on our lives, we can generally recognize patterns of destruction that are unique to us as individuals. Often, those areas that make us uncomfortable are the very places God wants to speak to us and teach us. He invites us to pay attention to those things that stir a strong inner reaction—even if it's shame—so that we might bring those hidden parts of ourselves into the light of His healing touch. But we do not look back for the purpose of taking on guilt; that would submerge us in another emotional tide pool. Keep in mind that feelings of condemnation are prompted by the devil, who constantly tries to withhold from our minds the full benefit of understanding that God's forgiveness is already ours.

Imagine this allegory with me for a moment. A Christian woman is racked with regret from the life choices she has made. Every day, she crawls to a pool where she thinks forgiveness can be found. But each time she gets close enough to slip into its healing waters, she is kicked backward. She has spent most of her life in the constant turmoil of inching forward a few feet, only to be shoved back again and again as an accuser says, "Don't forget your guilt."

Finally, the woman dies and goes to heaven. When she stands before Christ, she tells Him she wasted her life on Earth groveling with feelings of failure, unable to accomplish her life purpose because of it. But then Jesus reassures her that her sins were forgiven all along.

Surprised by His response, the woman asks, "Who kicked me to the curb every day in shame? The devil?"

Jesus looks lovingly in her eyes. "No, my beloved. It was you. Your own thoughts turned you against the truth. All Satan had to do was inflame your emotions. You did the rest."

Surely, we don't want that to be our story when we pass from this earthly life into the glorious heavenly realm and stand before the throne of Christ. God created us for so much more than that!

When we consider this woman crippled by fear, we realize with shock that our emotions can be such thugs! We don't have to blame others for kicking us when we're down; we do it to ourselves, repeatedly. But every time we engage in penitence for sins that Christ has already forgiven, we are exercising mutiny against the work of the cross. When we refuse to forgive ourselves and let our self-condemnation run rampant, we invalidate the beauty of forgiveness and push away God's healing touch. Punishing ourselves with thoughts of guilt and shame is in essence saying the punishment Christ took for us was not enough. It becomes a law we impose upon ourselves; we must pay to be acceptable.

The scriptures give us great clarity about this: "I do not treat the grace of God as meaningless. For if keeping the law makes us right with God, then there was no need for Christ to die" (Galatians 2:21). One of the hardest things we can do in this life is to learn to extend grace to ourselves.

With this said, we reflect on our past behavior patterns for the sole purpose of allowing the Spirit to guide us into the cultivation process of new responses and God-centered thinking for our future. These thoughts will hold spiritual objectivity. In other words, when we are too close to the damage, we can't see beyond the wreckage. But when we step back with the Lord and look through fresh eyes, God can reveal harmful patterns in our behavior. This can be likened to a bird's-eye view, a higher view than our own. For instance, when we look out at our yard through our back window, our eyes might meet a fence with a few broken planks, and we wonder what happened. A bird, however, looks down and sees the broken planks—and the tree that fell on the fence from another yard. When it comes to our emotions and the potential damage they cause, a bird's-eye view gives us higher objectivity.

I use this analogy because it casts light on an important spiritual principle. Looking upward first is the only way we can then look down on the landscape of our brokenness with acuity. As it says in scripture, "Lift your eyes to the heavens; look at the earth beneath" (Isaiah 51:6). This verse is crucial to our understanding of healthy thinking. Spiritual perspective never comes from a horizontal view. We must first look up. It's from this vantage point, standing with our eyes lifted up, that we find ourselves on the holiest of ground. As A. W. Tozer says in *The Pursuit of God*, "Lift your heart and let it rest upon Jesus, and you are instantly in a sanctuary." We stand in the presence of the Holy Trinity, who helps us look at our lives and the world around us with new eyes and fresh vision. We see this in scripture as a theme that points to where true healing flows. For instance, "As Moses lifted up the bronze snake on a pole in the wilderness, so the Son of Man must be lifted up" (John 3:14). If you are familiar with the Old Testament story in Numbers 21, you will remember that a number of people were bitten by poisonous snakes, but only those who lifted their eyes to look at the bronze serpent Moses held up were healed. This story of healing is so powerful that the emblem of a snake on a pole is still used in the field of medicine.

Of course, scripture is speaking of our salvation as we look to the cross, but the rescue of our minds works the same way. When we have been bitten by the venom of poisonous emotions, only looking to Jesus can bring true healing. We can study the scriptures all day long and come up with formulas to deal with rogue emotions, but our efforts will eventually fall short if we don't also lift our eyes to the Lord. Implementing the horizontal and vertical thought bubbles we talked about earlier in the book is another practical but spiritual way to employ the exercise of conversing with the Lord as we seek a higher perspective.

The "spaghetti model" used to predict the path of a hurricane gives us another good analogy. It shows the various computer projections of the potential paths a hurricane might take. The lines look like spaghetti strands, hence the nickname. Each gives a possible outcome based on speculative wind factors and atmospheric pressure.

We can imagine our emotional life on a map with the same theme in mind. For instance, if I had sent the first (harsh) draft of my letter, it would have been like a spaghetti strand projecting huge damage fueled by the wind of intensified emotion, and the result would be great relational breakdown. However, in the second scenario of waiting, praying, and rewriting the letter from a calmer state of mind, the spaghetti strand took an entirely different direction, one with less damage and with actual productivity. My friend was able to receive my prayer-filled and carefully worded concerns. This caused less strain to the relationship, and healthy boundaries were drawn. It is the difference of our emotions striking others at a category-one hurricane versus a category three—or perhaps even a category five.

But keep in mind that just because we make the effort to wait a reasonable response time does not automatically guarantee a smooth outcome. It does, however, mean a response has been thoughtfully and prayerfully executed above emotional impulse—and that is success itself. Responding in kindness, even when not reciprocated, can be rewarding, especially when we choose not to be offended because we are doing it for the Lord's sake rather than whatever the offender has or has not done to us.

Whatever you do, work heartily, as for the Lord and not for men. (Colossians 3:23)

Being extra aware of the propensity of emotions to cause damage will remind us to lean on the Spirit more than we normally might do. As broad and in-depth as a bird's-eye view or a spaghetti-model map, the Holy Spirit's perspective is beyond compare with immeasurable comprehension into every aspect of the trial at hand. The job of the Holy Spirit is to touch us at the deepest levels and guide us to the right track into *whatever is pure*. But we must be willing to give Him the authority to be the strong and mighty wind that directs our path. This means allowing His influence to become more important than the emotions we might be feeling in the moment. This takes looking up.

When I was about to make impulsive decisions, my husband used to say to me, "Honey, I will support any decision you make, but let me share with you some possible outcomes." I listened as he offered various projections, and it made a difference. This is a small, limited example of the Holy Spirit's ability to counsel us and help us reason through our emotional ambushes if we will simply allow Him the freedom to do so.

## Learning to live with—not within—emotions

With the Holy Spirit's help, despite our wildly disruptive emotions, we can experience the stabilizing effects of *whatever is pure*. Much like in the movie *A Beautiful Mind*, we can become alert and aware of those emotions that call out to us from tide pools we do not want to be in. This true story of a brilliant scholar who is experiencing a progressive case of schizophrenia offers exceptional insight. His mind becomes filled with imaginary people who relentlessly pressure him, which leads to an inevitable breakdown in his life. He eventually realizes that the only way he can function in the real world is to recognize the imaginary people when they appear and to ignore their urgings. Even though they continue to taunt him, he no longer follows their promptings. He learns how to live *with* and not within the emotions provoked by their voices. This is a turning point in his life, an observation of the past to successfully navigate into the future.

What about us? Do we want to continue getting stuck in the same old tide pools and making the same mistakes, or do we want to go in a new direction? Are we tired of responding in the same ways that keep us on the path of continual breakdown? Or is it time to allow God to change the course? We will never be able to completely eliminate the pressure of bullish emotions. But as we allow the Spirit to touch us, He will lead us on a new journey of responding differently. We will learn how to recognize damaging or crippling emotions, and though they attempt to pressure us, we can draw boundaries whether they leave or not.

It is important to note these boundaries will be for us—not for them (wayward emotions). They are for our safety to remind us not to cross over into unhealthy thinking, no matter how much we're provoked by them. We often make the mistake of assuming boundary lines are to keep difficult emotions out, and when that doesn't work (it never does), it feels like a tsunami breaks over our hearts, crippling us. That's why rethinking this is a crucial step of restoring health to our minds. Because difficult emotions are a regular part of everyday life, we must realize it's futile to try to extinguish them all. Instead, our goal must be to draw a boundary line around our response for our own well-being.

My continuing struggle with inner ear problems underscores this reality. Further testing revealed that an intricate part of the ear called the utricle was malfunctioning. In layman's terms, this meant I was seeing everything with a tilt. A horizontal line was now registering in my brain as angled. This small impairment caused my world to be on a constant slant. It felt as if I were in a carnival fun house that was not so fun. Have you ever noticed the sticker on your car's side-view mirror that says objects may be closer than they appear? It's similar to that. Simple things such as stepping off a curb became difficult to navigate because I was unable to perceive walking surfaces properly. For a season, I became fearful of going anywhere. The sensation of spinning that accompanied the onset of vertigo came and went, but the annoying feeling that the world was tilted was ever present. For me to live an active life, I had to come to terms with this tilt because it was my new reality. I needed to draw a boundary around my response to the heightened emotions that accompanied its presence. So, in time and with focused effort, I learned to ignore the emotions that tried to lure me to retreat and hide, and I began journeying outside more. I had to learn new habits to gauge distance and depth perception and to explore life differently.

Imagine a difficult scenario from your life. Perhaps something is broken and is not fixable or is not fixed yet. It could be a relationship, health issue, or work-related struggle. But whatever it is, for now it is here in your life, a part of your daily reality. Emotions provoked by this hardship may be pressing you to feel defensive, threatened, desperate, or despairing. Now, try imagining the boundary line of not allowing yourself to react in the same old way. Then, go one step further and ask the Holy Spirit to give you a new response and new perspective. Play this out in your mind, and you will instantly feel a sense of peace that is not ordinarily present. The emotional taunting hasn't changed, but your resolve has. You have allowed the Spirit to take you by the hand and walk you through an attempted emotional overthrow.

This unfolded for me when my mother died. I was overwhelmed with grief and constantly tried to find avenues to make the pain go away. My emotions didn't get better until the Lord impressed on my heart to stop trying to wriggle out of the pain. God reminded me that it was His plan all along to take my mom to heaven while I was young. It was the *whatever is just* road He was calling me to travel, and the heartache was a part of His bigger picture for my life. The pain and loss were to be a part of my story. When I finally grasped this reality, I was able to live with these strong emotions without living in them and operating from them. Instead of overthrowing me, they coexisted and became a part of my journey of allowing the Holy Spirit to lead me deeper into the fullness of dependency on Him. Drawing a boundary line around my response to an ever-present emotion (or tilt) finally allowed me to move forward.

What pain and loss are you facing? What is in your life right now that is keeping you under the dark clouds of broken thinking? What transitions and trials are part of your story? Have you sought the Holy Spirit's hand in leading you through them? You may have dealt with the issues in your life in various ways just trying to extinguish the emotions involved. But maybe, just maybe, you are called to walk through it. Perhaps it is intended to be a part of your story. Take a look at your life from a higher perspective, and allow a new framework of healthy boundaries so that you can be led through the storm of emotions quietly and with stillness of spirit. Grasping this perspective is life altering, but let's keep moving forward and tap into even deeper wells of emotional healing.

*Questions to Ponder:*

1. Has guilt or any other emotion been bullying you? How has it affected you?
2. Can you imagine two different spaghetti strand directions to a problem you are currently facing? What would the result of each direction look like?
3. Can you describe a boundary placement needed in your life to keep rogue emotions from luring you into a tide pool?

# Whatever Is Pure
## Part Four

～

NOW THAT WE HAVE ASSESSED that real damage can occur from emotional ambush, identifying triggers is key. We probably have no idea how much past difficulties overflow into our lives as adults. For instance, if we were verbally abused as children and therefore struggled with feelings of inferiority, those same emotions can be activated randomly in our adult lives. Simple things such as hearing a raised voice can trigger this. It could even be the positive noise of neighbors being excited to receive visitors, yet the volume and intensity provoke old, latent feelings that bring on a type of posttraumatic tide pool of emotions.

This is called a trigger. We all have triggers, and they're different for each of us. When you read about the various pools of thinking in chapter 2, you probably quickly felt the rise in emotions that your particular trigger brings. Once we identify what prompts these old feelings, we can be on alert to recognize them as we sense them rising. Pausing in these times allows us to prayerfully contemplate our emotions as data.

It may seem baffling how pain from the past continues to hurt us so deeply. But actually, it makes sense. The knowledge that they are real wounds from the past helps us understand why they are still present. In one way or another, there was a deficit of nurture in our early childhoods. This gaping absence made a huge opening for the rushing wind of emotion to swoop in. Going back to the trigger of yelling, we can note the lack of gentleness in a formative season of life. Because our emotional needs weren't met at a young age, a great sense of deprivation was carried into the future. These dark times are usually no longer present except in our memories, and sometimes not even our conscious memories. Yet, if we don't invite the Spirit's influence into the present situation that is triggering us, we will be dragged back to the past and experience those emotions as if they were still happening.

The kind of deprivation I'm describing is the absence of healthy emotional support or nurture that underscores all types of brokenness. We have natural defaults as humans to deal with these kinds of empty places, but they only make things worse, not better. Many times, we scramble to fill the void with worldly validation, or we overcompensate to seek approval. Sometimes, we run in an effort to escape and anesthetize. Then, there are times when we become self-destructive and give in to the lie of a faulty emotion. In this scenario, we actually become a victim to the emotional deprivation. Believing or embracing crippling emotions always makes us a victim. However, taking charge of our triggers takes us out of the victim's seat, and that is empowering.

Another important fact is that one emotional trigger can attract multiple emotional triggers from our past. Their ability to come together in a dark time is almost magnetic. Going back to the trigger of yelling, we can see how this works. There is a great sense of shame when we remember being scolded and berated. In the midst of feeling shame, other infractions come to mind—perhaps feelings of desperation that resulted in pleas for validation. This reminds us of how we were bullied, and that makes us angry. On top of these mounting emotions, we feel guilty because of the various ways we handled these situations. This one trigger of "shame" caused several other emotions to flood in—desperation, anger, guilt—and sweep over us, causing a phantom emotional overthrow. This can easily turn into a phantom emotional crisis. Even though nothing bad may be happening, it certainly feels as if it is, and it provokes the same emotional breakdown to our psyches. One small trigger can cause an avalanche of dark moods and feelings that we often can't readily explain. We may have described it as having a dark day or being in a dark place.

## *Spiritual poverty opens the door to great riches*

We might be surprised to discover that spiritual poverty is not the enemy. In fact, the Bible reveals that those who are in poverty are more able to experience the riches of Christ's love:

> Listen, my dear brothers and sisters: Has not God chosen those who are poor in the eyes of the world to be rich in faith? (James 2:5)

Great riches are hidden in poverty. There's the word *hidden* again, like a secret treasure from heaven. We think we are poor when, in fact, we are rich with potential for Christ's infilling.

The problem comes when we allow the emotions that have always accompanied our poverty to fill the void in our spirit and languish there. Remember, it is in this way that we often quench the presence of the Holy Spirit. John of Kronstadt, a nineteenth-century orthodox priest, was quoted as saying to a poverty-stricken, broken man on the street, "You were meant to house the fullness of God." What a marvelous truth to consider in the middle of an emotional ambush. God longs to fill the void with His loving presence and the weight of His truth. We must bring those barren desert areas to the healing springs.

This is the beautiful miracle of the power and presence of the Holy Spirit. Divine fountains flow where spiritual activity is found, whether it is through praying, scripture reading, meditating on truth, listening to a spiritual teaching, or singing worship songs. As soon as we engage in any spiritual activity, a sacred spring begins to well up inside our minds. Darkened clouds can't help but give way to sunny blue skies. It is not about the activity itself but the One whom it connects us to. The activity is nothing but a conduit to the Spirit so that we may be moved and touched by His presence.

As we draw close to Him, He draws close to us and becomes the well we drink deeply from. Consider the following scripture:

Call to me and I will answer you, and tell you great unsearchable things you do not know. (Jeremiah 33:3)

It is the kind of access that can be had only in personal receptivity and not in ritual. In the original language, the word *unsearchable* means "being inaccessible." It is *hidden*, reserved for personal intimacy and lavished on our personal poverty.

Consider an area of spiritual poverty and emotional deprivation in your past that is being carried into your present. Can you identify the crippling emotions that are occupying this void? This is an unhealthy tide pool, and it is snuffing out the life you are meant to live now. Not salvation, because that is eternally safe, but the abundant life you were designed to live while on Earth hidden in Christ. Triggers and wayward emotions keep us focused inward, staring at our poverty. They turn off the light that allows us to see the kingdom activity going on all around us. There is so much more that God wants us to see, hear, feel, and sense outside these triggered walls. It's time to keep these emotions from faking ownership.

All that is from above, all that is true, all that is just, all that is honorable, all that is pure, all that is lovely, and all that is praiseworthy is the opposite of poverty. In Jesus, we find an abundance of wealth that never runs out—riches overflowing with unconditional love, forgiveness, mercy, and grace. In fact, the more we take, the more there is. There is no need to worry about poverty ever.

It is the Spirit's delight to lead us into the depth of these treasures for mental and emotional well-being. It is part of the sacred journey that has been planned since the beginning of time. Jesus's work on the cross procured our redemption of the soul; that's why He was able to say "It is finished" before He died.

The Holy Spirit, however, did not say those words because His dispensation had just begun at the cross. He is at work even now moving upon our minds, bringing ongoing sanctification and healing. God knows that the world is a broken place that breeds broken thinking. He has come to rescue and lead us to spiritual health, not scold us or pass us by to seek polished people for His team. Consider Jesus's words in Mark 2:17, and let them bring healing refreshment to your mind: "It is not those who are healthy who need a physician, but those who are sick; I did not come to call the righteous, but sinners."

When the Spirit moves on us touching our wayward emotions, our tide pools turn into deep oceans of *whatever is pure*. Scripture gives us a description of what this looks like:

> But the wisdom from above is first pure, then peaceable, gentle, reasonable, full of mercy and good fruits, so all unwavering, without hypocrisy. (James 3:17)

Did you notice the first identifier? The verse starts out by telling us that the wisdom that comes down from heaven is first pure. Here is again the *whatever is pure*. It's not emotionless but rather anointed with the oil of the Spirit. This allows for the other attributes to follow beautifully: peaceableness, gentleness, reasonableness, mercy and good fruits, unwavering, and without hypocrisy. Something completely otherworldly happens to our emotions when they are touched by the weight and light of God's truth. Others can flail their arms in opposition all they want; it won't take away the peace from the person who is under the influence of the Spirit. It is like refreshing water that flows down from heaven on an emotionally weary mind.

The purifying effect can be noticed in our thinking immediately. Sure, wayward emotions may still be present, but they are comforted and defused by the Lord's presence. We feel the gentle leading that blankets us with heavenly reason, and it stirs in us a connectedness to God, His kingdom, and ultimately His bigger picture. We are filled with the Spirit, and the outflow manifests itself in His character evident in us. There really is a gentleness and reasonableness about it; it truly is full of mercy and good fruits.

I started chapter 2 with Psalm 23 to help us recognize that we are currently part of a kingdom realm that is active and alive. I mention it again as a reminder that the Great Shepherd of this kingdom wants to journey with us while we are on Earth. Even in the darkest valley, He will not only be there, but He will lead us if we let Him. Maybe you are feeling as if it's time to allow Him to lead you through your personal valleys of emotional ambush.

*Questions to Ponder:*

1.  Can you identify an emotional trigger that recurs in your life? What about a phantom crisis? Are you able to trace the different emotions involved?

2.  Can you identify the personal poverty associated with that trigger? How do you typically handle posttraumatic tide pools? Do you over compensate, anesthetize, or fall into a victim mentality?

3.  What conduits help you draw close to God to richly fill your personal poverty? (These can be reading books about spiritual growth, singing, praying, listening to sermons, spending time alone, taking walks in nature, listening to encouraging podcasts, and listening to or singing praise and worship songs, to name a few.)

CHAPTER 6

# Whatever Is Lovely
## Part One

⎯⌒⎯

*I*MAGINE THAT ONE OF YOUR dearest friends is fascinated with a particular destination. Everything she owns, from furniture to her walls' decor, is themed with this place in mind. As much as you care for this friend, her travel choice just isn't your thing.

And then one day, she passes away unexpectedly. You notice that your feelings about her favorite adventure spot change. You actually want to travel to that place and spend some time sightseeing there because it will remind you of her unique personality. It's interesting how, in an instant, something can go from being unremarkable to lovely, taking on a new and meaningful beauty all its own.

In a similar way, as we travel deeper into God's marvelous truths, we begin to see things differently about the spiritual realm that surrounds us. Things that we never noticed before become vibrant and alive, revealing hues, shapes, and fragrances of kingdom realities. Instead of our faith being the black and white of theology and adherence to rules, it becomes a colorful and aromatic exploration of relationship, a true love story of the soul. It is at this juncture in our journey that God unveils *whatever is lovely* to the mindful kingdom traveler.

In the Old Testament, we get a glimpse of this kind of loveliness radiating from Abigail when she meets David for the first time. Something different exudes from her that is notably otherworldly. It doesn't matter that David is on a tirade; after a conversation with Abigail, his angry mood is defused. That's because while David was consumed with earthly revenge, Abigail's mind was filled with eternal thoughts and realities. Her actions were a much-needed balm to David's anger.

Previously in this story, before David met Abigail, he requested provisions from Nabal, her wealthy landowner husband. Nabal in turn hurled insults at David through his messengers. David was so infuriated that he gathered his army and headed out to slaughter Nabal's entire household. When Abigail got wind of this, she immediately loaded donkeys with food and drink to meet David on the road before the bloodshed. As soon as she saw him, she dismounted her donkey and bowed down before him. When she straightened, she looked deep into his eyes and shared great words of wisdom with him.

Her speech was not filled with flattery, only the simple truth of God's plan for David's life and future (1 Samuel 25:28). David had encountered the loveliness of God's kingdom reality through Abigail. And like a tall glass of water in a parched desert, Abigail's words hydrated David's spirit. It reminded him who he was—his purpose—and the direction he was meant to go.

What about us? When people come in contact with our lives, do they see the loveliness of God in and through our thinking? We have distinguished in the previous chapters that this kind of spiritual mind-set does not come easily and is not automatic. Just as the physical life needs water, food, and sunlight, the spiritual mind also has its own culture of health.

Satan knows it requires daily maintenance for our renewed, spiritual mind to thrive, so he does everything he can to keep us from good spiritual thinking. One of the ways he wages warfare on us is to keep us stuck in our old culture of unhealthy broken thinking. This may be worry, preoccupation, anger, doubt, suspicion, anxiety, or anything else that churns our hearts. He doesn't care. He'll use any method to starve our minds of the life-giving sustenance of the Spirit. This is one of the reasons we are told not to forsake the fellowship of believers. We need each other. We must continually remind one another of who we really are—our purpose—and the direction we are meant to go, just as Abigail did for David.

Cultivating a healthy kingdom culture where we can journey through this world as like-minded pilgrims seeking a heavenly objective is at the heart of a Christian community. This may vary and look different from church to church and Christian to Christian. But it looks categorically different, in terms of shared experiences, from our secular lives where all our concerns focused on the old, the temporal and worldly, and the nondivine.

To be a part of the new life and culture means we must make a departure from the old when it comes to our minds. We could describe this as a cultural revolution that plays out in our lives daily. A sociologist once quoted by Ravi Zacharias explains cultural revolution as "a decisive break from shared meanings of the past." Breaking free from the bondage of broken thinking is a vital part of this cultural revolution. We were once driven by thoughts devoid of kingdom perspective, but as we've sought deeper connection to Christ, we've become immersed in a new culture with a different kind of thinking. If your heart is seeking to journey into a more expansive view of God, you will immediately be able to relate to this.

## A culture of renewal

The mind is a fascinating instrument. It affects us emotionally and physically. I once attended a class that taught the subject of medical studies on the brain. In one test group of people who had been emotionally traumatized, CT scans showed cloudy areas in their brains. After repeated counseling sessions, new CT scans on the same patients revealed that these cloudy areas had mysteriously disappeared. This kind of extensive testing was done to help people who have been subjected to trauma, addiction, and abuse.

What surprised me the most was when the instructor announced the greatest areas of improvement were seen in people who developed a pattern of regular prayer and meditation. He was not endorsing religion, but he did recognize that the transformation was undeniable. I don't know about you, but this revelation excites me. It is scientific proof of the power of renewing the mind.

Can you imagine what our brains would look like after extended time with our Almighty Counselor exchanging our old way of thinking for His new one?

The word *new* in this context is not just any kind of new. It conveys a new beginning, a brand new genesis for the mind. In the Greek lexicon, *kainos* (or "new") is described as coming from a new source, the enlivening source of the Holy Spirit. Therefore, it produces a new, qualitatively different ability to think in a way we were not capable of beforehand. This is not just good thinking but divine thinking, a kingdom mind-set, a spiritual world-view. The phrases found in our focus passage—whatever is true, honorable, just, pure, lovely, and praiseworthy—are all rooted in this kind of new, each a precious treasure of life-giving thought. God is instructing our minds to dwell in these places, to fix, reckon, and think on. And there is great reason for that. Dwelling, as the brain scan revealed, produces change. A. W. Tozer puts it this way in his book *The Pursuit of God*: "These are truths believed by every instructed Christian. It remains for us to think on them and pray over them until they begin to glow within us."

## The good fight of faith

So begins the good fight of faith talked about in I Timothy 6:12: "Fight the good fight of faith; take hold of the eternal life to which you were called." Keeping our minds in a pattern of dwelling in the new is the battle. Old wounds, old reasonings, old fears, old triggers, old regrets, old standards, old ambitions—any kind of broken thinking is poised to keep us from grasping this qualitatively different mind-set and clinging to it with all our might.

This requires loosening our grip on destructive thought patterns so our hands are able to take hold of the new, life-giving ones. This can be difficult because our old mind-sets have been our constant companions for so long. They are the ones we are familiar with, slip into easily, and hang on to tightly. But in reality, this old identity is in conflict with the new life God has transferred us into. We are a new creation with some bad habits of old thinking—not the other way around. As Christians, we don't fight for victory; we fight from a standpoint of victory. Each day, we must put on the armor of God to renew and strengthen our minds to think on or rediscover what already belongs to us.

Because most Christians mistakenly assume we must put on spiritual armor to battle for something we have yet to win, there is great need for clarification. Remember, our real-time connection as daughters and sons of God seated in the heavenly realm with Christ is filled with kingdom benefits that we have immediate access to while we sojourn on Earth—including the armor of God, which has been divinely designed to help us stand strong on a ground that is already ours.

This spiritual battle is not about losing our ground but about conquering the occupation of our thoughts by the enemy. A host of unseen influences continually strategize and campaign to throw off our spiritual equilibrium. They want us to chase after a hope of victory—as if we don't already have it. We think there is something wrong with us, when the truth is that Satan is behind this perpetual onslaught of manipulation. He conspires against us daily to mentally and emotionally keep us from the fullness of the inheritance that already belongs to us as children of God. The blue skies already belong to us; we must simply press past the dark clouds to take hold of them.

Are there really unseen forces plotting and planning against us to derail our thinking and crush our spirits? A well-meaning Christian once told me that fear of the invisible world was a sin. He was addressing my fear of the paranormal. He was right about me being scared but wrong about it being a sin to have a healthy fear of it. In fact, a pastor at the time told me, "If human eyes were opened to see the invisible realm, we would all be sickened with the terror at the reality of the demonic underworld that lurks around us." It would scare the wits out of anyone! What's more, these entities thrive in an environment of broken thinking. Our old mind-sets actually invite satanic activity. Yikes! That's where our armor comes in. It is made to protect us from a dark, supernatural realm.

## Fighting with zeal

A cultural revolution in the area of our thinking happens when we purposely decide the new is where we want our minds to dwell. Knowing that it won't be easy, we determine to fight for it. With that said, we recognize the incalculable need for the individual pieces of armor that give us powerful defense against being drawn back into our old patterns of broken and limited thinking. The truth is that there is so much more, an entire kingdom realm that we are connected to where new thinking can flourish. But because the devil works hard to keep this truth shielded from our minds, we must press into the kingdom with sheer determination. Notice how the scriptures encourage this:

> Brothers and sisters, I do not consider myself yet to have taken hold of it. But one thing I do: Forgetting what is behind and straining toward what is ahead, I press on toward the goal to win the prize for which God has called me heavenward in Christ Jesus. (Philippians 3:13–14)

The word *press* in the original language means "reaching out or stretching toward." There is no such thing as stagnant faith; either we are pressing on toward God, or the world is pressing in on us. Either we are pressing into the light, or the darkness is pressing into us. Either we are reaching into the new, or the old is stretching after us.

A commonly overlooked passage tucked away in the gospels sheds light on our plight in this Christian journey. I warn ahead of time that the way it reads may cause us to think it's talking about evil people being violent toward the kingdom, but it's the opposite. It's actually an eagerly seeking people laying hold of the spiritual realm. Take a look at Jesus's words:

> From the days of John the Baptist until now the kingdom of heaven has suffered violence, and the violent take it by force. (Matthew 11:12)

When we understand the original meaning behind these words, we are given fresh inspiration to reach toward the kingdom. The words *suffered violence* mean "to press in with energy." When people heard about Jesus, they came to see Him, and they did so with great gusto and determination, sometimes even lowering sick people on mats through their roofs. Can you imagine the effort it must have taken to hoist this man up to the housetop and lower him down with precision? The words *and the violent take it by force* mean "to seize upon." Those people were not going to let anything stop them from taking hold of God's kingdom promises through Christ. The violent person in this context has an energetic mind and obstinate faith. Some might call it spiritual moxie. Those who reach, stretch, and earnestly press in toward spiritual things will reap spiritual benefits.

In my season of vertigo, this reality of violently pressing in became very real. When my unhealthy ear sent aberrant signals to my brain, the first step was to be still to calm my fears and anxiety, but the next step was an aggressive call to action. Restful passivity would not do. If I were to get better and regain my balance, I would have to go after it with sheer determination. Let me tell you, this was not an easy feat. But my physical therapist informed me that it was necessary. Her prescription was for me to begin the vigilant exercise of "fixation." This meant that even though the room looked as if it were swaying, I needed to find one place in the room and keep my eyes fixed on it. Once I located that spot of fixation, I was to inform my brain repeatedly that the spot was not moving as I focused on that spot and walked toward it. This essentially retrained my brain with true information.

It's no surprise that the New Living Translation of the Bible uses this word *fix* in our passage of focus: "Fix your thoughts on what is true, and honorable, and right, and pure, and lovely, and admirable" (Philippians 4:8). The Bible makes us aware that a spiritual war is going on for control of our minds. Satan continually causes aberrant emotions and thinking to propel our world to spin out of control. Our first order of defense is to be still and recognize that God has new thoughts for our minds that are true. These truths become our fixed places of focus. The next step is action: we must fight with energy, eagerness, and holy audacity, taking hold of truth and informing the unhealthy areas of our lives of its dominion—over and over again until we believe it, because it's already true.

Questions to Ponder:

1. What old kinds of thoughts seem to reach toward you with the most vigor?

2. A cultural revolution means purposely deciding the new is where you want your mind to dwell. What kinds of new thoughts are you inspired to reach toward with spiritual determination?

3. Can you identify an area of thinking where you have been passive, waiting on God, when really it requires energy and action on your part? What truth would you fix your mind on and repeat over and over until you've changed your old thinking into a brand new mind-set?

# *Whatever Is Lovely*
## *Part Two*

⌒

OULDN'T IT BE LOVELY IF we didn't have to deal with broken thinking anymore? There will come a day when darkness will disappear. But until then, we live in a broken world where the old continues to dominate us if we let it. Putting on our spiritual armor is a vital part of reversing this process so that we may press in toward the kingdom of God with great success. Let's look at what the scriptures have to say about this divine battle suit designed specifically for the believer:

> Put on the full armor of God, so that you can take your stand against the devil's schemes. For our struggle is not against flesh and blood, but against the rulers, against the authorities, against the powers of this dark world and against the spiritual forces of evil in the heavenly realms. Therefore, put on the full armor of God, so that when the day of evil comes, you may be able to stand your ground, and after you have done everything, to stand. Stand firm then, with the belt of truth buckled around your waist, with the breastplate of righteousness in place, and with your feet fitted with the readiness that comes from the gospel of peace. In addition to all this, take up the shield of faith, with which you can extinguish all the flaming arrows of the evil one. Take the helmet of salvation and the sword of the Spirit, which

is the word of God. And pray in the Spirit on all occasions with all kinds of prayers and requests. (Ephesians 6:11–18)

## Belt of truth

The first item we are told to put on is the belt of truth. The Greek word *aletheia* means "truth as unveiled reality lying at the basis and agreeing with an appearance." In other words, is what's portrayed on the outside coinciding with what's really going on in the inside (heart and mind)? We are not being true to ourselves when our professions of faith do not influence our thinking. When our actions are simply a mask and are not truly representative of how we feel or believe, there's a gaping hole in our spirit.

Cracks will eventually show if we don't really have faith in the theology we are attempting to live. A practical example can be seen when we assert that God finds us valuable, but then we secretly berate ourselves for being worthless and unimportant to anyone. It might be our squeamish behavior and inability to accept a compliment that gives us away. We applaud when we hear of God's favor for the underdogs of this world, but now God is challenging us to believe this about ourselves. Girding ourselves with the belt of truth means it's time for this spiritual fight to get personal.

Because of our human brokenness, there are all sorts of discrepancies in our minds between truth and actual belief in that truth. As we take up the armor of God, closing the gap between what is truth and what we believe about that truth will have a great impact on how we wage spiritual warfare.

Recognizing that we may not believe fully in various parts of our lives is the first step. This is something God desires for our hearts—that is, truth on the inside: "You desire truth in the innermost being, and in the hidden part you will make me know wisdom" (Psalm 51:6).

Note the word *hidden* here in keeping with the theme of hiddenness we find in the scriptures. It is this hidden place of the heart that God wants truth to reach. This brings us back to the belt of truth. In this imagery of a soldier in battle, we glean better understanding. In the days of old, a tunic would have flapped all over the place if it had not been secured by a belt, especially during battle. Likewise, our minds are also prone to trip us up in battle unless girded by truth.

For instance, we may confidently proclaim the Lord's control over all our circumstances yet find ourselves scurrying to take control as we are flooded with worry and anxiety—like loose-hanging fabric flowing in multiple directions at once. That's because we really don't believe it. So many variables and influences cause our feelings to pull us in different directions—namely, our old culture of broken thinking. Believing or putting our faith in the truth is the only thing that has the divine power to bring all our fraying fragmented thoughts together and hold them securely in place.

But how do we get to that place where our minds can be touched with truth at the deepest level? It helps to think in terms of going beneath the hypothetical layers of our being. For instance, imagine taking away the layers of your identity, one by one. First, take away appearance, then talents, then position, then preferences, then possessions, then political beliefs, then connections, then cultural influences, then circumstances, then status…what's left? Who are we after all that is removed? What do our naked souls look like?

That is who matters to God, not all the other things. God loves and cherishes the person inside, the simple you, the person who is born with nothing and dies with nothing. God wants to reach that person with a truth that anchors the mind and influences behavior organically. It supersedes all layers of life and is meant for the most intimate part of our souls. God has always been near to that person, the person we are at the core of our being, but we can't always feel His presence because of all the other layers that have piled on us over the years.

The following scripture confirms this reality: "The Lord is near to all who call on him, to all who call on him in truth" (Psalms 145:18). Sometimes, God allows circumstances to bring about a shedding of layers to help us get to this place. Have you ever noticed how intimacy with God seems to happen during intensified events, such as catastrophes? A wise person once said that a crisis was a golden opportunity to share the good news because the fences people naturally build around themselves come down during those times.

It's not just during intensified times we see this happening but intentional ones as well. About twenty years ago, my husband and I began an evangelism ministry in our local church for kids. Our daughters participated right along with us. As the children gathered for service, we invited the visiting kids to a special room for a gospel presentation. We found that because they were separated from their own life layers—peer pressure, self-consciousness, and the distractions of their chaotic home environments (for many of them)—they were open to the truth. And not only were they open to it, they soaked it in because they felt nearer to God. The setting intentionally inspired a sense of sacred weight.

When we talk about nearness to God, it is not a physical nearness, because God is everywhere at all times. Remember, God is outside of time and space, so He is not limited or bound by our definition or perception of those. Nearness in the divine sense is found in spiritual receptivity. God may feel far away, but His nearness is felt by those who draw close to Him in truth—beneath life's layers.

Because it's a human tendency to forget His presence and all that comes with it, the belt of truth is necessary. Day after day, we sit stewing in anxiety at the clouds of darkness that surround us. But greater is the reality of light that is in full force behind it, a mighty weight of unstoppable light.

If we could peer into the spiritual realm, we might very well see that an entire army of the Lord is with us. We are given reminders of this kind of presence throughout scripture. For example, in the Old Testament, a servant of Elisha's became frightened when he saw that an army had surrounded the city. The prophet Elisha comforted his fears by telling him not to be afraid because God's unseen army was even bigger. After Elisha prayed that his servant's eyes would be opened to the truth of this unseen reality, "the Lord opened the servant's eyes, and he looked and saw the hills full of horses and chariots of fire all around Elisha" (2 Kings 6:17).

Time and time again, we see the heavens open up for our benefit so that we might be encouraged that the battle ultimately belongs to the Lord—including our daily battles. When we press in toward truth, the tides turn from doubt and discouragement to faith and hope. His power is greater than the trials we face, and His kingdom is more alive. Once again, we are reminded that we're part of a grander design than we realize.

Esther caught hold of the truth and bound it around her waist as she faced the king in what she feared would result in certain death. She recognized her purpose being of heavenly origin and acted on it—standing in the gap for her people.

Likewise, God used Abigail as divine intervention during a season of darkened thinking for David. Despite the fact that she, too, faced potential death, Abigail shared with him the loveliness of kingdom realities. We, too, belong to a chosen and set-apart people-group that expands history. Even our duration on the timeline of life has been ordained. We get only a fraction of time here on Earth, but it's directly connected to a bigger plan.

Putting this belt on (figuratively) helps us pull together all those random frayed feelings of purposelessness and ties them together with the sacred sash of a higher calling in life. We begin to recognize a pattern: even though a weight of darkness looms big, the weight of light is bigger, grander, and infinitely more powerful! The results are stunning as we see a winnowing out of the old from the new.

Just as God hovered over the waters in Genesis 1, separating the darkness from the light, putting on the belt of truth binds our minds to the new, closing the gap between truth and what we really believe about it. We may have previously thought in one way, connected to our old cultures, but today we are choosing to think in another, exchanging a darkened thought for a hopeful thought—one that is true.

What is dragging you down? Take that thought to God and ask Him to replace it with confidence in Him. For instance, instead of succumbing to any thought that this thing or that situation is impossible, embrace the reality that in Christ all things are possible. As you do this throughout your day, you will find it life changing.

As we move forward looking at the various pieces of the armor of God, keep in mind that they are all truth. Receive them with great energy of mind, seize upon them, take them in, put them on—they are yours.

## *Breastplate of righteousness*

The breastplate for war in the biblical era covered the vital organs, specifically the heart. In times of spiritual battle, we must remember that Christ is the breastplate that stands between our flawed hearts and judgment. We are humans with flesh and blood, and the heart of our emotions is a prime target. The divine breastplate of righteousness covers our humanness, our limitations, our failures, our blunders, our emotional overthrows, and ultimately our inability to live victoriously apart from God's grace, which is now ours. This is an amazing piece of armor for all believers. But for those of us who are haunted by our own brokenness and weakness, it is pure gold.

Meditate on this reality: Jesus perpetually stands between us and the stone throwers of this world. I'm going to say it again for emphasis: Jesus perpetually stands between us and the stone throwers of this world. He is our breastplate of righteousness!

We are God's holy and beloved children, not because of anything we have done but because of what He has done. His righteousness belongs to us now. We receive it based not on our goodness but on God's. That is why it is so important to have this piece of armor in place mentally. It already belongs to us whether we have it in our minds or not, but the mental placement serves us well in the battle of our thinking.

Otherwise, when brokenness overcomes us, we may find ourselves melted into puddles of insecurity, shame, and feelings of worthlessness. Ultimately, this is where the devil targets us, whether he spurs on our own self-loathing or it is prompted by others. Walking throughout our day while being aware of this breastplate brings about a cultural revolution that gives us tremendous courage and hope in something greater than our own efforts. We are wearing God's credentials, not our own. We find that even in our frailties, we are God's treasured children. He delights in being patient with us because it brings a weight of glory to Him rather than to us. Notice how the scriptures affirm this in 1 Corinthians 1:27–28: "God has chosen the foolish things of the world to shame the wise, and God has chosen the weak things of the world to shame the things which are strong, and the base things of the world and the despised God has chosen." Therefore, although we are flawed, we are highly valued and lovingly covered.

## Good-news shoes

Next, we have our feet fitted with the good-news shoes. This part of our spiritual armor reminds us that God has prepared us for the walking part of our journey, even as we step into difficult seasons. Our ability to tread shaky paths in our lives is a direct result of the gospel of peace that belongs to us regardless of our circumstances.

There is a saying that goes like this: "Everything will be OK in the end. If it's not OK, it's not the end." Grasping this truth brings solid hope, even if hope seems impossible in the "in-between" times—like the dismal day the disciples experienced between Jesus's crucifixion and resurrection. On that darkened day, the disciples felt a great weight of hopelessness. All they could see were dark clouds of discouragement, confusion, and pain. Our divine footwear is designed for those days—to carry us through to the other side into the light and power of the resurrection.

God was always with His disciples, even when they could not feel His presence. The same is true for us. God promises that He will go with us no matter what the road looks like. As the good-news shoes cling tightly to our feet and uphold each step we take, so is Christ bound to us. We never walk difficult roads alone, even when we feel alone. Paul experienced this personally when everyone deserted him: "At my first defense, no one came to my support, but everyone deserted me. May it not be held against them. But the Lord stood at my side and gave me strength" (2 Timothy 4:16–17).

The Roman soldiers wore a leather sandal-boot with hobnails in the soles that dug hard into the dirt. Much like the cleats football players wear to hold sturdy ground while being tackled, spiritual shoes can cleave deeply to spiritual soil. Likewise, with our good-news shoes, we will find ourselves able to walk the heights and depths on Earth. Even if we are intimidated to travel certain roads, God has prepared our shoes for the paths we will walk.

Consider one or two transitions you are facing. Imagine those as mountainous trails you are called to scale. What trouble does the thought bring to your heart? If it is fear, then take your spiritual shoes, dig them into confidence in God's protection, and stand firm. Imagine yourself doing so. Is there a scripture that comes to mind? Step boldly into it, and begin to walk.

Remember, these specialty shoes are meant to go in only one direction, and that is toward the Holy One. Focusing on the giants in our lives is natural, but to walk toward the light, we must turn away our gazes from the darkness of crippling emotions. Fearing the future or looking back, holding on to bitterness or staring at regret, focusing on sin or failure—all of these immobilizing emotions must be rejected.

As I was praying and considering this piece of armor, I was reminded of a time when I had a supernatural encounter while driving in my car. I've never had something like this happen before, and it never happened again after. I was a young adult traveling by myself across the country and ended up taking a wrong exit, which I didn't realize. It was late at night, and I kept driving deeper into the darkness. The farther away from major highways I traveled, the blacker the sky became until eventually there were no more streetlights or signs of life. All of a sudden, I heard a deep voice flood the car: "Turn around, and go back." A sense of fear and awe came over me. Of course, I turned the car around immediately and headed back, only to discover I had taken the wrong road.

I can't help but think about the parallel of our journey in the Christian faith. Our daily destination is our communion and fellowship with Christ in His kingdom mind-set. Satan causes us to take the wrong exit through our emotions and jaded thoughts because he wants us to travel deeper into the darkness away from true fellowship or spiritual signs of life. Then, God gently reminds us not to keep walking toward the darkness but to turn our face to the light. It's as if the Father says, "Turn around and walk toward me. Come on, you can do it. Stop walking toward the dark." When we do, we find our feet move steadily with the gospel of peace—step by step—confidently taking back the mental ground the enemy has sought to steal from our minds.

> For God, who said, "Let light shine out of darkness," made his light shine in our hearts to give us the light of the knowledge of God's glory displayed in the face of Christ." (2 Corinthians 4:6)

We must use our gospel shoes to turn toward Christ if we are to see the face of Christ.

Securely fitted shoes are crucial. Mental preparation means to have great confidence to address our difficulties, the rocky road before us, the tragedies that have befallen us, or the transition we are in because God has ordained special footgear for the journey. This correlates with what we discussed in chapter 3, "Whatever Is Honorable." Making time for sacred silence in which to meditate on God's sovereignty in our circumstances helps us slip off our earthly footwear in order to strap our good-news shoes securely in place.

The "wow" of God has the power not only to clothe our feet but to lift them to unprecedented heights over the roughest terrain. The leading of the Spirit will take us along routes that divinely lift our emotionally wearied hearts. Remember, there is more to the story. An end to the hardships is in sight, a place where our joy will be made full. We are a part of a cultural revolution that is spiritual and requires spiritual attire.

## Shield of faith

We are also told that we must be ready with the shield of faith to block the fiery darts of the enemy. Imagine a soldier standing behind his shield to deflect the arrows aimed at him. This is what happens when we stand behind our shields of faith in the spiritual realm. The shield is not penetrable, and the arrows that are aimed at us strike the shield instead and fall away to nothing. Without this shield, however, we would be struck, and the flesh hurts when struck.

When our faith is weakened, we can be struck over and over again. These daggers are meant to provoke the old culture of thinking in our lives. Picture daggers filled with the flammable substances of hurt, disappointment, jealousy, anger, bitterness, envy, doubt, and fear. Can you remember feeling struck in this way where an emotion suddenly seemed to ignite? The term *fiery darts* gives a good word picture of what that looks like. The devil kindles our emotions, and he isn't satisfied until we are completely engulfed in flames.

When considering the shield of faith, we must ask ourselves if we are trying to be our own shields. Self-help is only temporary and very flimsy. A good friend told me that for a season when facing a difficult trial, she would not allow herself to cry. It didn't change what was going on inside her heart, and after a time of forcing herself not to weep, she became physically sick from months of holding back tears. Tears are God's design to help deal with emotional hardship. Medical studies support this fact. Researchers have discovered that chemicals built up in the body during stress are actually removed by tears. My friend became worse off for trying to be her own shield. Once we identify these man-made shields, we can make a prayerful mental transfer to God. We must never trust in our own strength. Even those good things in our lives that build confidence need to be traced back to God. After all, what do we have that God hasn't given us? Our ability to fight the good fight of faith has been given to us by God, too. Children have it right in trusting easily and eagerly, which correlates to our *whatever is just* discussion of cultivating a childlike faith.

## Helmet of salvation

The helmet of salvation guards us from being completely annihilated by doubt. Oh, the cleverness of the devil, that he would mess with our minds in this way. He throws marbles of doubt under our feet as we walk the difficult paths of life in hopes that we slip and hit our heads in failure, and we do. Yet with the helmet of salvation securely in place, though we misstep and fall flat, we shall rise again strong and sure footed in the grace that has been secured on our behalf. It's not about falling; it's about rising by the power of God even when we fall. "For though the righteous fall seven times, they rise again" (Proverbs 24:16).

Even nature tells the gospel story of resurrection, like the day itself. The sun sets in a shroud of darkness, but morning brings the light of its glorious rising. Scriptures touch on this beautiful spiritual principle: "His mercies begin afresh each morning" (Lamentations 3:23). It's the rising of mercy. When we fall on our heads, and we will, the helmet of salvation gives us the ability to rise in divine deliverance. There is rescue after rescue available to us each day as we embark on our spiritual journey in the kingdom culture to which we belong, with a never-ending reservoir of new starts. New mercies greet us each morning with a blank page to write a fresh story, one that speaks of truth, faith, and hope. We are washed clean, and nothing can separate us from God's forgiveness. The battering of doubts will come, but we are safe, our helmets are on, and we shall see salvation in all its glorious splendor.

## Sword of the Spirit

Next, we are told to take up the sword of the Spirit, which is the word of God. Digging into the word does several things. It redirects our hearts, hushes our worries, and inspires our thinking for the pilgrimage we have been called to. It demonstrates to our own hearts a sense of priority, meaning, and purpose. Through His word, God breathes into us great knowledge and understanding into the spiritual realm we are a part of. I'm not referring to black-and-white ink on paper but rather Jesus, the Living Word, who communicates who He is through the Spirit, bringing the written word to life in our hearts. The Living Word is able to cut through falsities that affront us daily, slicing through old thinking masterfully like a divine machete, clearing the brush of the world's values and standards from our sacred path. This mind-set correlates with this chapter—whatever is lovely—which we will look into in further detail in the coming pages. God's word brings clarity to those things that He finds lovely and pleasant to His sight, lovely places that bring Him joy. And discovering what brings joy to God will strengthen us, "for the joy of the LORD is your strength" (Nehemiah 8:10).

Do you need strength? Then allow this hidden truth to come alive in your heart. Seek what brings God joy, and you will be strengthened. These things are often contrary to the world's ideals, and to really sense this loveliness, one must allow a spiritual circumcision of the heart by the blade of God's word. The power to bring about a cultural revolution of epic proportions is found in allowing God's illumination to cut away the old thinking, which gives us the divine ability to be sensitive to the leading of the Spirit into new thoughts found in kingdom activities. It also prepares us for the encounters of our daily lives, providing for others from the bounty of truth we have received that day—a spiritual slice of bread ready to hand out to those who are hungry for truth. This is exactly what Abigail was able to deliver to David. Walking into our day with the sword of the Spirit gives us a divine sense of equipping to meet the needs sent across our path.

With all these things, we are told to pray in the Spirit, which mysteriously unites the material world and the spiritual world. Prayer is the transcendent union of a human request with the divine ear of God. It is where the visible and the invisible intersect in great force. The Spirit, as we discussed in the last chapter, is the enlivening and empowering of Christ on a personal level. It is the most sacred communion with Christ, the leader of our new culture. He is the Good Shepherd who guides us on our sacred journey here on Earth. He can lead us into intimate knowledge of His kingdom and bring it to life in our hearts in ways we may never have imagined possible. He is pleased to share His eternal truths with those who draw close to Him.

Acts of self-disclosure and kingdom revelations are reserved for those who are seeking a deeper union and connection with Him personally. This is where our relationship is experiential, going beyond the knowledge of the mind to an intimate bonding of the heart. Even those who come from a solid church background will find the difference palatable between the culture of church and the kingdom culture of otherworldly thinking that comes from a personal connection with Christ.

The spiritual benefits of the armor of God are vast, but one thing they all have in common is the health they bring to our thinking. Moving forward in this book, we will learn how this applies to our minds and subsequently our lives.

*Questions to Ponder:*

1. Do you recognize an area in your life where there is a discrepancy (a gap) between what you proclaim to be true and what you really believe about that truth?
2. What giants (difficulties, turmoil, struggles, transitions) are in your life? What scriptures can you dig your gospel shoes into in order to keep your eyes on the face of Christ while turning your eyes away from these giants?
3. Name emotions specific to you that have a tendency to ignite when provoked.

# Whatever Is Lovely
## Part Three

⌐◝

W E ARE INVOLVED IN A personal ongoing cultural revolution for a new and life-giving way of thinking, one that is not meant for the distant future but for right now, today. It is a wonderful part of our lavish and never-ending spiritual inheritance. In this section, as we delve deeper into the depths of whatever is lovely, we will see this culture take spiritual shape in our thought-life and translate into a heavenly aroma. As our new mind-set blossoms and blooms, so does the fragrance it emits, and it will be countercultural to our old ways of thinking.

The scriptures speak in terms of the aroma of Christ in many places. One that stands out is Psalm 45:8 because it is a prophetic writing about Jesus: "All your robes are fragrant with myrrh and aloes and cassia; from palaces adorned with ivory the music of the strings makes you glad." Here we get a picture of the absolute delight to the spiritual senses that are attached to the man Jesus, whom the world did not esteem: "He was despised and forsaken of men" (Isaiah 53:3). We marvel at the contrast that Christ is a lovely fragrance to some but not to others. To those who know Him in the spirit, there is something so fragrant about the humble, meek ways of Christ—the fragrance of heavenly royalty.

In the Bible, we observe the opposite by the religious leaders (Pharisees) who were blatantly at odds with the jubilee expressed by others when Jesus was in their midst. Only the heavenly hosts were privy to this weight of glory, as well as those for whom God had opened their spiritual senses. For instance, Jesus's mother was turned away by the innkeeper and forced to give birth in a lowly barn surrounded by bugs and animals, but the shepherds, wise men, and angels celebrated His birth. "And suddenly there appeared with the angel a multitude of the heavenly host praising God and saying, 'Glory to God in the highest, and on earth peace among men with whom He is pleased'" (Luke 2:13–14).

It's interesting that the God of the universe would bring His son into the world in such a crude and inelegant manner—so unimpressive, inconvenient, and uncouth. We may be familiar with some of these disadvantages in our own lives. Yet because Jesus is our Savior, we are a part of this royal fabric that conveys the aroma of His otherworldly kingdom. Make no mistake about it, though the world dismissed the arrival of this baby king, the entire spiritual realm highly esteemed this pivotal day hidden in this unimpressive manger moment. It is similar to the type of heavenly celebration that occurred the instant you and I became believers: "I tell you there is rejoicing in the presence of the angels of God over one sinner who repents" (Luke 15:10). This is sheer loveliness scented of heaven.

To truly grasp the magnitude of such hidden beauty, we need a complete change in the landscape of our thinking. As we progress down this anointed path, many of our own manger-like moments will come alive as our thinking is transformed, and we will have opportunities to recognize their fragrance daily. These moments may seem unimpressive in the flesh to the casual observer, but the aroma of the Spirit is evident to those who are seeking things above.

I remember one of my own manger moments when pregnant with my fourth child, Kaitlin. A dear friend had just lost her three-year-old daughter to cancer at the time. Celebration of my new pregnancy naturally took a back seat to the grieving that was permeating the small town where I lived. There was a solemn quiet, no baby shower, and no fanfare. There was a loneliness to my special season, yet I was drawn into a unique closeness with my unborn baby and was in tune with God's presence and delight. When my daughter was born, there was a sacredness about the experience, one that was not dependent on the celebration of others, one I will never forget.

It's easy to miss the manger moments as we go about our busy lives. Mine happened out of necessity, not because I chose it. Manger moments smell of death to the self-life, and that is why they are often overlooked—even in the church. But look at how Matthew 5:3–11 describes the beauty that accompanies some difficult circumstances:

> Blessed are the poor in spirit, for theirs is the kingdom of heaven. Blessed are those who mourn, for they shall be comforted. Blessed are the meek, for they shall inherit the earth. Blessed are those who hunger and thirst for righteousness, for they shall be satisfied. Blessed are the merciful, for they shall receive mercy. Blessed are the pure in heart, for they shall see God. Blessed are the peacemakers, for they shall be called sons of God. Blessed are those who are persecuted for righteousness's sake, for theirs is the kingdom of heaven. Blessed are you when others revile you and persecute you and utter all kinds of evil against you falsely on my account. Rejoice and be glad, for your reward is great in heaven, for so they persecuted the prophets who were before you. (Matthew 5:3–11)

Notice the conditions mentioned in this passage that are regarded as blessed. Wouldn't these typically be considered unfortunate circumstances by the world's standards? But in these verses, God is painting a portrait of what He deems valuable and lovely, and it is stunningly at odds with what the world deems admirable. The world promotes illusions of peace and prosperity; it brokers ideas of happiness and positivity in things that do not bring fulfillment.

To think positively by the world's standards is to think happy thoughts whether they are real or not. But "blessed" thinking is dwelling on the divine realities that are true and that never change, even in difficult circumstances. In fact, the heart-wrenching difficulties of life deepen our awareness of blessedness. Embracing the beauty of these poverty-stricken places of the heart is the same as opening the gardens of our minds to be watered by the very water of life, Jesus. And when we do, our kingdom thinking becomes aromatic and pleasing to the Lord. We become spiritual blooms in His kingdom garden.

Jesus personified humility as He walked the earth leaving a trail of heavenly fragrance wherever He went. He is our role model when it comes to loveliness of the mind, and not only a role model but the very source of our very own transformation. The word tells us we are to cultivate the same mind:

> Let this mind be in you, which was also in Christ Jesus, who, being in the form of God, did not consider it robbery to be equal with God, but made himself of no reputation, taking the form of a bondservant, and coming in the likeness of men. And being found in appearance as a man, He humbled Himself and became obedient to the point of death, even the death of the cross! (Philippians 2:5–8)

Notice the clear directive in the beginning of this passage: "Let this mind be in you." What mind? That "which was also in Christ Jesus." This truth is a wellspring of divine illumination into the blueprint of God's design for our minds. It is both lovely and fragrant, and it brings Him great joy.

Let's take a closer look at some of the phrases in this verse and unpack the weight of light meant for our thinking as we sojourn toward a renewed mind.

### "Did not consider it robbery to be equal with God"

In this phrase, which means not needing to prove equality with God, we see in Jesus the mind of meekness and lowliness. He did not need the recognition of men. This was evident in the way He constantly tried to silence those who wanted to make Him a political or public figure. Fame had no appeal to Him. His living conditions were modest. His occupation was unassuming. His ministry on Earth was carried out in lowliness and meekness of heart. There was no campaigning, no fundraising, and no advertising. He had no interest in building a personal brand. He knew who He was, to whom He belonged, and the purpose for His earthly journey.

Consequently, He was continually disregarded, passed over, and unrecognized as the long-awaited and prophesied Messiah. A crown of thorns was placed on His head to mock Him as an unlikely king despite His miraculous but quietly humble ministry and lifestyle, which the religious leaders had observed for three years.

The world considers meekness and lowliness signs of weakness. Humility does not meet the secular standard of success. The world seeks and applauds the opposite—power, prestige, position, and control. In doing so, they miss out on the holy fragrance that accompanies a meek and gentle spirit. We see these secular characteristics slip into the church as well. They look impressive and are often cloaked in polished performance. But all the charisma and magnetism in the world will never be lovely or fragrant.

Behind every selfish ambition is Satan's pride-centered agenda. He is the embodiment of the character traits that are the antithesis of Jesus. That doesn't mean we may not be in a position of prestige or financial advantage in this life; there were certainly many biblical figures who were. The difference is that we recognize that wealth does not make us any more valuable than anyone else. Paul said he considered all things rubbish in comparison to shaping a kingdom mind-set. He was intentional about cultivating a different kind of wealth.

I'm not talking about a mind-set bent on putting ourselves down to appear meek; that is false humility—a facade, a mask that covers the hidden pride beneath. Truth is the unveiled reality at the basis of and in agreement with an appearance. So, when we are self-deprecating, we are admitting that we don't believe the truth of our inner value in Christ. By the same token, conforming to superficial values, striving to impress, proves we don't truly believe that what God values is enough. A. W. Tozer gives us a balanced, sober word for personal estimations of the human condition: "In himself, nothing; in God everything."

As believers, we are called to a cultural revolution infused with a new way of thinking. There is a fragrant loveliness in letting the same mind be in us that was in Christ. When you think about genuine lowliness and meekness connected to faith, who comes to mind? That person is exhibiting *whatever is lovely.*

"But made Himself of no reputation"

In this phrase, we see in Jesus a humble heart and mind; He was the embodiment of true humility. Having a disregard for the vain things of this life, Jesus did not allow the impressive things of this world to become His banner or platform.

Anything that is not of humble means brings attention to itself. We see it on every level and in every realm, especially in social media, whether it's promoting, posting, tweeting, and so on. The world lives to exhibit its glory by publicizing information that says, "Look at me!" Jesus, knowing this and wanting us to cast our attention on something greater than the glitter of this world, emptied Himself of any reputation so that we might see the weight of glory in the eternal value system of the living God.

Isaiah 53:2–3 describes Jesus this way:

He has no form or comeliness; and when we see Him, there is no beauty that we should desire Him. He is despised and rejected by men, a man of sorrows and acquainted with grief. And we hid, as it were, our faces from him; he was despised, and we did not esteem him. (Isaiah 53:2–3)

The truth is that we are not contributing anything of true value to the kingdom of God if people are drawn to the glare of our reputation, status, or any other earthly gain. Inflated images and egos are a disservice to God because they cast an illusion of false glory and false light. Remember, Jesus chose to have nothing in this world so that His confidence would be in God alone and the spiritual kingdom He is building. He chose to be poor for our sakes, even though He was very rich. "Though He was rich, yet for your sakes He became poor, that you through His poverty might become rich" (2 Corinthians 8:9). As we seek the same mind that was in Christ, who made Himself of no reputation, we will blossom with a sense of otherworldliness. His kingdom priorities will be a fragrant part of our life, and the aroma will touch those whom God sovereignly allows to cross our path.

"Taking the form of a bondservant"

In this phrase, we see that Jesus's heart and mind were always to put others' spiritual well-being first, to the point of serving them with His very life on the cross. Behold our perfect example! Christ is our perfect role model. "While we were yet sinners, Christ died for us" (Romans 5:8).

The word *servant* in the Bible is also described as "underrower," the very lowest of positions assigned on a boat, down below where it's hot and laborious. How appropriate is this term for being a servant of Christ. As Christians, we are called to serve down at the bottom of the boat where it gets the hottest. Many Christians today miss out on this privilege. It's desirable to hobnob on the top deck with those considered the A-listers of the Christian culture. But in God's economy, the one who sees humility as the goal is on to something beautiful. James gives us a snapshot of what that looks like: "Pure and genuine religion in the sight of God the Father means caring for orphans and widows in their distress and refusing to let the world corrupt you" (James 1:27).

In Paul's letter to the Corinthians, he warns of getting caught up in the celebrity Christian culture that the world affirms. He even goes so far as to contrast the difference between superficial Christianity and the genuine deal:

> For I think that God has displayed us, the apostles, last, as men condemned to death; for we have been made a spectacle to the world, both to the angels and to men. We are fools for Christ's sake, but you are wise in Christ! We are weak, but you are strong! You are distinguished, but we are dishonored! To the present hour we both hunger and thirst, and are poorly clothed, and beaten, and homeless. And we labor, working with our hands. Being reviled, we bless; being persecuted, we endure; being defamed, we entreat. We have been made as the filth of the world, the off scouring of all things until now. I did not write these things to shame you, but as my beloved children, I warn you. For though you might have ten thousand instructors in

Christ, yet you do not have any fathers; or in Christ Jesus I have begotten you through the Gospel. Therefore, I urge you, imitate me. (1 Corinthians 4:9–16)

Paul describes himself as a spectacle, fool, weak, dishonored, hungry, reviled, persecuted, and defamed, the filth and off-scouring of the world. If we can wrap our minds around the true value of being included with Paul in this category, our service to Christ can't help but bloom with otherworldly fragrance. This is the hidden blessing of discovering that our top calling is found at the bottom.

There's that word *hidden* again, reminding us of the golden theme of the countercultural kingdom to which we belong. It's evident when we run across this kind of servant's heart in a Christian. It's not the false humility that looks for ways to inadvertently brag about serving; it's the generous, quiet heart that sees every opportunity as a willing act of service to God. As Christians, we have the same opportunity to live out our faith in willing service to others, not because we have to but because it is an act of love toward God, who has freed us to do so. It doesn't matter if we are beggars on the street or if we live in a mansion; we have the same opportunity to serve with the mind of Christ.

"And being found in appearance as a man, He humbled Himself"

In this phrase, we see in Jesus the heart and mind of sacrifice. His sacrifice in the world's eyes was great—in fact, baffling. How could the King of kings sacrifice the palace, the throne, and the crown for the humble position of a carpenter with no home to call His own? Doesn't everything in the world belong to Him already? And if He had chosen to, could He not have had whatever He wanted, including what we would rightly consider appropriate kingship, kingdom provisions, and surroundings? Absolutely!

The scripture declares, "For the kingdom is the Lord's, and He rules over the nations" (Psalm 22:28). And of Himself, He says, "Everything under heaven is mine" (Job 41:11). But Jesus reminds us, "My kingdom is not of this world" (John 18:36).

In the world's eyes, the grander you are, the better you are treated; the richer you are, the greater you are served; the higher your position, the more your privilege, and all these things are your rights. The Lord's example is completely contrary and turns this kind of thinking upside down. He gave up rights to what was rightly His to be born as a human baby, grow up like any other boy, work as a humble carpenter, and serve the people in an earthly ministry that brought mockery and disdain more than praise. He gave up the heavenly palace, the crown, the prestigious gatherings, and all the things that typically accompany being a king.

Imagine what the world would look like, and how fragrant it would be, if Christians followed Christ's example in this—not just sacrificing for sacrifice's sake but seeing the things of this world as less valuable than God's kingdom. Moses demonstrated this kind of commitment to the unseen dominion of God. He gave up all the privilege that came with being raised in luxury as an adopted son of the pharaoh to follow God's true calling on his life.

> By faith Moses, when he had grown up, refused to be known as the son of Pharaoh's daughter. He chose to be mistreated along with the people of God rather than to enjoy the fleeting pleasures of sin. He regarded disgrace for the sake of Christ as of greater value than the treasures of Egypt because he was looking ahead to his reward. By faith he left Egypt, not fearing the king's anger; he persevered because he saw him who is invisible. By faith he kept the Passover and the application of blood, so that the destroyer of the firstborn would not touch the firstborn of Israel. (Hebrews 11:24–28)

It is amazing to think about the level of personal sacrifice it took for Moses to give up a royal position on Earth to be associated with a different type of royalty altogether, a heavenly royalty that held no earthly dignity. His fragrant sacrifices would yield eternal kingdom benefits. Moses was building and collecting treasures in heaven that would never fade or rust.

Because Jesus chose this position of humbleness rather than palace life, He was not a leader whom people admired or aspired to emulate. If we are honest with ourselves, we often make the same mistake in our interactions with people. We admire those who impress us, the bold and assertive, and we overlook the meek and mild.

But there is a loveliness that surpasses all the impressiveness of this world, one that expands inwardly and does not give credence to outward superficiality. As A. W. Tozer once said, "To be great outwardly and small within is a kind of hypocrisy, but the modesty that hides a spacious interior under a simple exterior must be most pleasing to God." The more we recognize this truth concerning our own lives, the more our days will take on the fragrant aroma of the man Jesus Christ. We will be conformed to His likeness, having in us His same mind, knowing that we are being fashioned and formed for "the city which is to come" (Hebrews 13:14). Oh, lovely citizenship!

*Questions to Ponder:*

1. Can you identify a manger moment in your own life, something of great value that might typically be overlooked by the world?
2. Think of someone who exhibits genuine meekness, not self-deprecation. What are some ways this meekness is evident in his or her life?
3. After reading through the character traits of the mind of Christ, what stands out for you? How does Jesus's earthly journey inspire you on your earthly journey?

# CHAPTER 7

## Whatever Is Worthy of Praise
### Part One

——◦——

LAUREN'S YOUNG LIFE DID NOT include traveling to exciting destinations, not even interesting local places that most kids got to visit. She was a small-town girl from a difficult background, and her experiences were limited to the area where she grew up. When Lauren turned eighteen, she got a part-time job at a local diner. She wanted to be a waitress, but because the manager was not impressed with her, he put her to work behind the scenes doing janitorial tasks. Regardless, she grew to know the menu from cover to cover. When the lead waitress called in sick one day, the manager reluctantly let Lauren fill in. She was a natural with people and treated everyone kindly because she knew what it was like to be rejected and looked down on.

At the end of that shift, there was one table left with a complicated food request. It happened to be the owner of the diner—a young, handsome man who stopped by twice a year to check on the business. He was quite taken by Lauren and impressed with her ability to place his order strictly by memory. Before long, he was visiting regularly just to see her. The manager became frustrated because the owner kept requesting Lauren as his waitress, and he had no intentions of giving her that permanent position. Finally, the manager contrived a reason to fire her and let the owner know she was no longer employed. But the owner tracked Lauren down at her new place of work. Long story short, they dated, fell madly in love, and eventually married. Imagine the shock on the manager's face when the owner arrived a few months later to check in on that old diner with his new bride, Lauren, on his arm.

When we hear stories like this, we naturally celebrate; after all, this is what great movies are made of. It's a classic heartwarming story with a Cinderella twist. The girl who had nothing in this narrative was given everything. She went from being discarded to being accepted. Thus, she was redeemed from the throes of rejection. But I must add a caveat here. A woman does not need a man (or a man a woman) to be rescued. The romantic in all of us, however, can't help but cheer when someone finds an empowering match. This is why movies are able to capitalize on such an endearing sentiment.

Lauren's story is all our stories. Oh, we might come from completely different circumstances, and it may have nothing to do with romance. But on some level, we, too, have faced rejection. Whether we have felt dismissed, thrown back, spurned, eliminated, brushed off, denied, overlooked, excluded, or anything similar, it hurts. To feel unwanted or disapproved of deeply wounds the psyche. Many difficulties in life can cause broken thinking, but rejection is one of the most debilitating. This is because it is the antithesis of what we were created for—our full acceptance in Christ. No wonder it's a method the devil uses so effectively. Rejection strikes us at the core of the nurture we were designed for. If rejection has played a major role in our life, it can be a great mountain of weight to conquer.

The word *rejection* in the original language of the New Testament means "to disallow." We see it used in the scriptures when describing the stone (Jesus) that the builders rejected (Matthew 21:42). The place in their hearts that rightfully belonged to Him was closed because they did not esteem Him worthy. They shut Him out. They disallowed His entrance to their own detriment. Yet even with this rejection, Jesus was able to live His life with full confidence in who He was in relation to truth. That didn't mean He didn't feel pain; in fact, He was called a man of sorrows, which means He had natural feelings and emotions.

Jesus, however, did not allow emotions to deter His resolve. Listen to His heart as he expresses sadness over the people who rejected Him: "O Jerusalem,

Jerusalem, the city that kills the prophets and stones God's messengers! How often I have wanted to gather your children together as a hen protects her chicks beneath her wings, but you wouldn't let me" (Matthew 23:37). We can take notice of three significant thoughts in this verse. First, it is not wrong to long for broken things to be fixed. "I wanted to gather your children together as a hen protects her chicks" conveys a pure longing and yearning, as from a mother's heart. "How often" indicates that He felt sadness on more than one occasion. "But you wouldn't let me" declares concession; it is an acknowledgment of a separation between what was desired and what was actually happening.

These wise words reveal an important principle for us to cling to when we are excluded, overlooked, rejected, or disapproved of. Longing for change, while conceding that a situation has not changed, allows us to move forward. If we do not come to a place of concession, we might stay stuck in an unhealthy longing, one that brings ongoing compromise.

Some people spend their whole lives wishing for and desperately seeking something that never comes, like the approval of a family member or friend. They feel as if that one piece of validation will make them happy, not realizing that their preoccupation with it is hindering all other relationships around them. We've all seen this happen in various forms—the friend who loses touch with those who care about her because she's so intent on chasing after a love relationship that remains out of reach, the man who loses his identity because of rejection, the fallout of the rejected soul whose life overflows with bitterness. Whatever the case, knowing when to concede is missing, along with an inability to deal with rejection, which breeds breakdown in other areas of life.

## When concession is missing

This breakdown can be observed in the relationship between David and his son Absalom in 2 Samuel 19. Absalom's heart turned against his father, and David became stuck in an unhealthy longing as a result. Even when David's soldiers risked their lives to keep Absalom from killing him, David showed no interest in their welfare. When Absalom died in battle, David went into deep, inconsolable mourning, causing the soldiers to retreat in shame as if they had done something wrong in protecting the king (2 Samuel 19:3). When the leader of the army saw what was happening, he warned David to stop neglecting the people, or they would turn on him. David's tunnel vision of not conceding to his son's rejection brought ongoing compromise to his own life and the lives of others.

Part of the difficulty in not conceding is that we internalize there is something deficient in ourselves, and we feel miserable about it. We yearn for validation to take away this feeling. But notice that Jesus's reaction to rejection didn't turn inward or speculate that something was wrong with Him. He did not neglect everyone else around Him or chase after the approval of those who looked down on Him. His Father's approval was all He needed, even in the midst of rejection.

Human brokenness makes our hearts work differently. Without understanding why, we exchange God's unconditional acceptance for the approval of a human being who is just as flawed as we are. In doing so, we give away the power that belongs to God in shaping our identity. We don't realize that our emotional well-being is being compromised. This progresses so subtly that sometimes years slip by before we are aware of its overarching influence in other areas of our lives.

How can we know when this is happening? One of the more obvious signs is when someone's influence becomes more important than God's influence in our lives. If their opinion dictates our behavior, we have transferred power to them that belongs only to God. The need for approval is a stronghold and can keep us running in circles on a wheel like a hamster seeking crumbs of validation. If we come from a background of deprivation in nurture, these tiny scraps may even seem necessary for our emotional survival.

Perhaps these words sound uncomfortably familiar. If so, maybe it's time to give yourself permissions to step off the hamster wheel so you can be all that God has intended for you to be in Him—regardless of the rejection you might be facing. Letting go of the pursuit of human acceptance and drawing closer to God bring great rescue to the mind. It's safe to be rejected by the world—even by those we love dearly—when we are highly valued by the

Lord. Our significance does not change when others reject us. Rejection does not define us. God does, and His opinion is all that matters.

## Coming full circle

As we come to the end of our time together, my hope is to bring us full circle through our focus passage of scripture found in Philippians 4:8. Our journey started out by examining how the outside influences of the world affect our minds in relation to God. Our journey concludes by understanding how our inner connections to God transform and rescue our thinking and, subsequently, our worldviews. This transfer from external to internal is pivotal to our spiritual health. As we consider our final focus phrase, *whatever is worthy of praise*, we will observe how the weight of spiritual intimacy brings ultimate healing to our minds. It can even rescue us from the throes of rejection.

Although Lauren's story is filled with hope, real and lasting freedom can be found only in the person of Jesus Christ. Embracing God's full, unwavering acceptance brings powerful rescue for the mind. Some people imagine that marriage will solve this issue, but it does not. As humans, we are flawed and unable to carry a happily-ever-after scenario into full reality. Even if it starts out well, death will inevitably bring an end to all earthly fairy tales. Temporal marriage, although precious in God's sight, is only a training ground for our eternal union with Christ.

This is the beautiful backdrop to *whatever is worthy of praise.* There will be no death or waning of love in the heart of our heavenly bridegroom. We don't have to settle for scraps because He has prepared a bountiful feast full of welcoming favor. Even now, we are connected in a way that brings life, new thought, and great celebration. Our souls have been saved, and our minds are in the process of being rescued. And if we let Him, God will continue this ongoing restoration, and it will be His joy to do so.

We have mentioned some beautiful locations in the preceding chapters, but nothing compares to the lush, peaceful, tranquil, majestic landscape of personal connection to our Lord and Savior. Journeying past the outer gates of brokenness, beyond the inner courts of rejection, we find ourselves walking straight into the presence of God's uncompromising acceptance. The veil in the tabernacle that was torn in two by Jesus's death on the cross bids us to enter. Discovering what our relationship looks like with God behind this mysterious veil—in the holy of holies—is what we were designed for. Each phrase in Philippians 4:8 is meant to usher us into this most divine space where our minds can flourish in peace, safety, and security. It's here behind this mysterious veil that we dwell in the perpetual favor of our beloved. Beyond the dark clouds of broken thinking, we find the bluest of skies. Now this, dear friends, is worthy of praise!

*Questions to Ponder:*

1. As you think about your life, can you identify a time of unhealthy longing from rejection because you did not concede? Can you describe how it affected other areas of your life?
2. Can you identify behaviors that reveal you have not yet conceded (e.g., pining, replaying the way it used to be, trying too hard)?
3. Has rejection ever caused you to feel deficient? Have you ever given away power to someone else's opinions? How could you handle that differently the next time you are faced with a decision?

# Whatever Is Worthy of Praise
## Part Two

⁓

RAISE IS AN EXPRESSION OF gratitude. The original Hebrew of the Old Testament translates it as "being mindful of God's favor," and the Hebrew word for thankfulness is *yadah*, which conveys a throwing down or casting down of praise. It is something that overflows in our hearts and naturally comes out; otherwise, it might burst. As Jesus said to the Pharisees, who told Him to quiet the crowd's joyful praising, "I tell you, if they keep quiet, the stones will cry out" (Luke 19:40). That's exactly how it works. It is a sweet celebration of the soul, and it can't be stopped! God's rescue brings praise! And praise is an integral part of the kingdom culture. In fact, the scriptures tell us that God is enthroned on the praises of His people (Psalm 22:3).

As important as it is to understand the weight found in the word *praise*, the word *worthy* brings our subject matter for this chapter into greater focus. Some things are truly worthy of praise, whereas others are not. For instance, there are things that garner adulation on a secular scale that are not worthy of praise on a spiritual scale. A person promoted at work may receive accolades, but it won't be the same as the fragrant praises that go up when a loved one turns to God from addiction. Although they both inspire competition for human attention, one is temporal, and the other is decidedly marked with the divine. In other words, the qualifying mark of being worthy of praise is identified by the good news of otherworldly rescue through faith.

The Bible is filled with narratives that tell of divine rescue meant to set the heart aflame. Jumping off the pages of scripture into our own life stories, we can see how redemption solicits praise. Our paths might be different, but we rejoice as each one radiates the good news of rescue.

It's the same with our minds, and it is not rescue from only bad thoughts but good ones, too. It is the difference between good thinking and divine thinking that can change the course of destiny. Good thoughts are fine, but spirit-led thoughts based on truth are life giving. They are something entirely different. Secular good changes with cultures, times, and opinions. And although impressive on the outside, such as worldly success, it always lacks the characteristics found in the passage of Philippians 4:8 because it is not divine. God's way for the mind, however, changes who we are on the inside and causes us to thrive and come vibrantly alive.

## Good versus best

When we first become Christians, the individuals we were before conversion are still prominent in our character traits. As we travel deeper in spiritual intimacy with Christ, that begins to change. Who we were gradually becomes secondary to our identities in Christ. In other words, our personhood and sense of belonging progressively change hands from ours to His.

We see how this plays out in the life of Sarah in the Old Testament. In scripture, we are told that Sarah was married to Abraham, and they were both in their old age. God promised Abraham that he would be the father of a great nation. Of course this meant having a child. Sarah waited and waited, but years went by, and she only got older. She tried to surmise how God could accomplish this when she was well beyond the age of fertility. Because Sarah was still very much her own person, independent from God, she shrewdly came up with a plan to hasten fulfillment of His promise. There was no ill intention behind her maneuvering, only earnest desire.

We all face this juncture in our daily lives when a decision must be made. Do we take matters into our hands when circumstances look difficult, thus choosing to act independently from God? If we do, then we, like Sarah, might be pursuing a secular good instead of waiting for a divine best.

Sarah might have considered her plan the equivalent of a modern-day surrogate. Sarai (as was her name at the time) talked her husband, Abram (as was his name at the time), into sleeping with their Egyptian slave Hagar. Hagar became pregnant, and in her haughtiness at this victory, she looked down on Sarai, who blamed Abram for her suffering. Trying to appease her, Abram gave Sarai permission to do with Hagar as she saw fit. Sarai mistreated Hagar, which caused her to flee. God appeared to Hagar in the desert and had mercy on her. He sent her back to submit to Sarai and have the baby. The entire situation was a mess fueled by emotional ambushes from all directions.

Fast-forward to many years later. God was about to implement His divine plan to bring forth a child from Sarai's dead womb. He appeared to Abram to go over the covenant He was making with him, and part of that was changing their names to Abraham and Sarah.

Have you ever thought about this interesting dynamic in terms of marriage? Traditionally, in Western cultures, the name changes for the bride. Marriage is a new covenant between husband and wife, and they become one. Our heavenly union is the same. We are called Christian because we are Christ's own. This tells of our belonging to Him and His heavenly kingdom while we sojourn on Earth. Our name is found in Him and represents a new destiny and belonging with divine purpose.

We find this to be the case for Sarah. Sarai was more dependent on making God's plans happen the way she wanted, but Sarah was dependent on God, trusting His way no matter what happened. On one hand, the desired outcome was on the throne; on the other hand, God was on the throne—regardless of the outcome. Intimacy was the catalyst. The same holds true for us when we face rejection or any other emotional tide pool. Either we allow the tide pool or rejection to crawl up to the throne in our hearts, or we give God that rightful place. Only one can reign.

When we recognize that we may have misplaced this power, a transfer of weight is in order. For Sarah and Abraham, there was a relational shift of trust. From this new union, faith took hold, and it looked different. Faith quiets our agendas and gives way to the Lord: "Be still and know that I am God." (Psalm 46:10) This kind of stillness is not passive; it takes great effort. It's the activity of waiting, of continually handing the plan back to God and trusting His development of it, even when it looks bleak or impossible.

Sarai coming up with a scheme on her own, no matter how clever, could never compare to the glory of God's way of accomplishing His higher purposes for Sarah. His divine method of bringing forth His plan would not be found in Sarai's "good" plan but through Sarah in God's "best" plan, and only then could it become worthy of praise.

Hundreds of years later, the apostle Paul draws the parallel of this narrative for us in the epistle to the Galatians: "It is written that Abraham had two sons, one by the slave woman and the other by the free woman. His son by the slave woman was born according to the flesh, but his son by the free woman was born as a result of a divine promise" (Galatians 4:22–23).

Let's pause to let that take root in our hearts—a divine promise. When it comes to our minds, God has a plan; it is part of His promise, which came to us through His promised rescuer, Jesus. Our plans make us slaves to our broken thinking, but God's plans are divine and meant to set us free. God beautifully threads His covenant throughout the history of the scriptures. He is more than a religion or theology. He is our perfect match, and we are united to Him in promise.

The very nature of the word *promise* garners great assurance. I remember when my husband and I were engaged, and I was feeling anxious about our future. Would this last? Would he fall out of love and leave me? He assured me with these words: "Paula, even if we should fall out of love, I am making a promise to be committed to you for the rest of our lives." No longer a slave to fear and manipulation of trying to keep a relationship from falling apart on my own, I was able to rest in his promise. There is something so binding and secure about a promise. Imagine embracing this kind of promise from God!

Whether we're pondering the lives of Sarah, Esther, Hannah, Ruth, Rebekah, or our own, we are all women connected to this promise. All their journeys led to the ultimate Promise Keeper; the promised seed, Jesus; the redeemer of our souls and minds. He has come like a knight in shining armor and brings never-ending benefits that are safely hidden in our divine betrothal. Our ultimate rescue comes in the form of spiritual intimacy that was planned from the beginning of time. Here we discover our truest sense of belonging. When the dark clouds of life roll in, and they will, we can remember this covenant connection that can't ever be taken from us. In fact, God has set His rainbow in the clouds as an ongoing reminder of this everlasting promise. The rejection of this world pales in comparison to God's rich acceptance, which never disallows our most intimate and sacred connection to Him.

*Questions to Ponder:*

1. Describe an area of your life where you attempted to go in a good direction rather than a divine direction.
2. Can you recall something from your past that held its place on the throne of your heart?
3. How would you describe your personal identity? Has that shifted as your intimacy with Christ has grown?

# Whatever Is Worthy of Praise
## Part Three

❦

OUR HEAVENLY CONNECTIONS BRING A new life that comes with many amazing privileges and benefits. Let me share an example in the temporal sense from my own earthly marriage. I was a single mom with four daughters when I met Jeff. He was a leader in the church and highly thought of. I, on the other hand, had many years of brokenness. There was so much mess in my background until my daughters were born, and then God moved heavily on my heart.

Several years later, Jeff came into my life, and we fell in love. He wanted to marry me and be a father to my girls. We instantly perceived the power of God's rescue at work and sensed the awe that began spreading through the people in the church. It gave hope to single moms everywhere. We did not realize how big this wonder was until people we didn't know stopped us in the halls and shared their encouragement. Being married to this man meant more than I realized. In an instant, I received his amazing name as my own and all that went with it—his sparkling reputation, his spotless credit—and everything that he owned belonged to me. Incredible!

But this is only a temporal reflection of our permanent union with God in a bond that is superior in every way. We are joined through a covenant made by His own blood. We would be forever lost if He had not given up everything to redeem us. We were broken, and He looked at us as if we were the most beautiful bride in the world. He made us alive in Himself and seated us beside Him in the heavenly realm, where we are operating out of a place of wholeness.

Everything that belongs to Christ now belongs to us—His reputation, His righteousness, all of it is credited to us. We have unparalleled access to what this means. We are completely loved with a love that never changes or dies, and it is unconditional. We don't have to do anything to earn His love. Jesus is our best friend and soul mate for eternity. If we could comprehend the weight of what this really means, we would spend the rest of our days walking on cloud nine.

## The superiority of experiential knowledge

This level of intimacy goes deep, far surpassing simple head knowledge. As we're told in Ephesians 3:19, God wants us to "know the love of Christ that surpasses knowledge, that you may be filled with all the fullness of God." Take notice that there are two words for knowledge in this verse. It says that one surpasses the other. The first "know" is *ginosko* in the Greek lexicon, which means "to know experientially." This is contrasted to *oida*, which means "to perceive with the intellect." God wants us to experience the kind of knowing where our spiritual senses come alive in fullness. It is to be acquainted with him personally and intimately. This word *know* is used in other parts of the scripture to describe marital intimacy. This depth of knowing is reserved for a special union of oneness, a sacred connection of heart where we are found hidden in Him as His bride.

This brings us to the last of our spiritual senses. Taste is the only one of our five senses where we become one with the object of our consumption. For instance, our minds feed on the living word and are nourished by its spiritual food, which becomes a part our being. This is presented eloquently by Christ in the imagery of His body being the bread and wine we eat in the sacrament of Communion. How fittingly intimate is this last spiritual sense. It is symbolic of our oneness with Christ and the life-giving force that accompanies it.

For many Christians, however, the enlivening of the spiritual senses is a foreign concept. Often, our relationship with God is limited to the knowledge of Jesus's death on the cross. But after the Crucifixion comes the power of the Resurrection. Our relationship with Christ does not conclude at the cross; it ignites and becomes enlivened by the Spirit. The Greek word in the scriptures that describes this phenomenon is *zoe*, which means "life and not just any life, but new life."

We named our youngest daughter after this beautiful word. Our hope for her was to thrive in the new life that awaited her soul, not just her birth. We knew an awakening to the unseen world was prepared for her. Although we would bring her up in an intellectual knowledge of God, only the Spirit could raise her up into an experiential life-giving union with Him. This would be the onset of a new and powerful life. Like Jesus when raised from the dead—a beginning, not an end—so is our journey into the beauty of His resurrection. In Him, we can walk in a way that triumphantly reflects our renewed mind. The Song of Solomon is reflective of our spiritual union with Christ, our heavenly bridegroom. Its verses convey the sentiment of our resurrected life in Him, beautifully summed up in verse 10: "Arise, my beloved, and come away" (Song of Solomon 2:10). Arise! Our beloved is telling us to rise up from all those layers of dead thoughts that have clouded our minds from old, broken thinking. Arise! Awaken! Journey with Him, and discover in Him the fullness of all your spiritual senses.

There is so much power here—resurrection power. Yes, hidden in the resurrection is great life-giving power. Listen to how Paul describes it:

> I also pray that you will understand the incredible greatness of God's power for us who believe him. This is the same mighty power that raised Christ from the dead and seated him in the place of honor at God's right hand in the heavenly realms. (Ephesians 4:19–20)

We will face difficulties while on Earth, but nothing can stop our hearts from soaring freely with our beloved as we awaken inwardly and taste the sweetness of His love.

## The physical versus the spiritual

This is where faith comes in—believing and trusting in something that profoundly reaches the hidden recesses of the inner person. As Hebrews 11:1 reminds us, "Faith is proof of that which is not seen." Therefore, true and living faith involves relying on the spiritual senses rather than the physical: *perceiving* the bigger picture, *listening* for His presence, seeking the *touch* of His Spirit, *smelling* the fragrance of His meek and humble ways, and *tasting* His love in personal fellowship. After all, physical sense is only a temporary shadow of the spiritual, which will be ours forever. Even now, we can sense Him moving on, whispering into, and touching the deepest part of our hearts. Our journey with God is spiritual and majestic. The physical world cannot compare to its glory.

God points out the difference as He compares Hagar and Sarah using the analogy of mountains. Hagar's mountain represents the temporal (nonspiritual), and Sarah's represents the promise (spiritual). Note the contrasts: "You have not come to a mountain that can be touched" (Hebrews 12:18, Hagar's mountain). "But you have come to Mount Zion, to the city of the living God, the heavenly Jerusalem" (Hebrews 12:22, Sarah's mountain).

Likewise, we have come to a greater mountain than the physical that bogs us down in this world, one that is superior in every way because new life is found here! The physical mountains we face on our earthly journey may seem more prominent and more demanding, but they will disappear someday, and all that will remain is the spiritual (verse 27).

Finally, we discover that we are meant to scale the mountain of promise, confident that God's delight in us flourishes there. Safe in His love high atop this lofty sacred summit, we learn how to respond rather than react to the world's rejection. We retrain our minds to choose our thoughts and actions proactively in light of God's truth.

After all, when it comes to rejection, we have been guilty, too. Our preoccupation with our own rejection has "disallowed" God's influence in the deepest part of our own hearts. He wants us to know and embrace His love for us, but too often we have rejected Him in pursuit of the world's validation. He adores us. Do we believe it? He accepts us and cherishes us, knowing everything about us. Does it make a difference? We will be able to tell if it does or not based on the power and influence it has on our minds.

We may have spent our days trying to manage our Christian lives independently without pressing in to Him intimately in a way that garners this kind of trust. Christ's sacrifice on the cross and redemption of our sins is nothing short of reversing this process and restoring God to His rightful place in our minds, putting Him at the center of our thinking. Only God can be trusted as the source of our identity. In fact, Christ is our identity. We have entered a union of oneness that can never be separated. We are bound to Him in every sacred sense, no longer two but one. This is why Jesus could say, "Whatever you did not do for one of the least of these, you did not do for me" (Matthew 25:45). In other words if the world *has not* valued you but has mistreated or neglected you, Jesus tells us it is the same as doing it to him. Amazing, as we take on His identity, He takes on our wounds. All rejections aimed at you have fallen on Him. When we enter into the fires of disapproval, He goes with us.

*God's love reaches the mind*

When I was young, I struggled with deep feelings of inadequacy, even as a Christian. It incited me to be rebellious and impetuous. I took nothing seriously. When I became pregnant with my first child, that all changed. Somehow, the knowledge of new life growing inside of me caused me to see everything differently. Simple things that I would typically overlook took on great value. There was a little person soon followed by four more little people whose lives mattered tremendously to me. It was remarkable that, while pregnant, I felt each child developing and growing, as well as my love.

Our relationship to God is like this. It is meant to come alive inside us and grow and develop. Our security and confidence in Christ are meant to blossom and bloom, but only if we allow His life within us to become more than just theology. We can be Christians for many years before our relationship transforms into an intimate, thriving reality that makes us glow. Imagine if we journeyed every day with the joy and contemplation that we are the treasured tabernacle where Christ's love dwells. Charles Spurgeon conveys it well: "Every Christian is a God bearer."

When my children grew up and moved away, I found myself at a crossroad of struggling to believe that the truths I had taught them about God's love were also meant for me. While they were with me, I had such strong faith, but it was because of them and for them. When my children were gone, my old patterns of broken thinking took hold, and I eventually realized I did not have a deep, abiding faith in the core of my being.

Sure, I believed in God, but did I really believe that God loved me—just me, not the mom me? I felt an identity crisis come on, one that took me to the depths of despair. Cracks in my faith became evident to my own heart in this dark season, and I was extremely unsure of my value. Rejection had always been a big tide pool in my life, and I just couldn't seem to shake it. I prayed and diligently sought relief from the scriptures but was still tormented. It was like a weight dragging me farther and farther down that darkened path of old. I felt unloved, even though there were many who loved me and expressed it beautifully. Years of failure and rejection had swept back over me. I was stuck behind a mountain of broken thinking—until God intervened.

I could feel Him leading me into a new season of rescue for my mind. But it was challenging because brokenness kept me from the healthy thoughts that God wanted me to embrace. My faith would need to be activated, since faith is the only thing that has the power to move mountains, and this one needed moving. Begging, of course, like Hannah for increased faith, put me on the right track. I began to recognize the worldly weights that were keeping me from moving forward. The spiritual kingdom became more and more alive to me, with greater purpose and meaning. I sought out places of sacred silence to incline my ear to listen. Whispers of good emerged out of the bad. I became aware of those emotions that kept thrusting me into the darkness, and I sought the help of the Spirit to lay hold of the new. One of the greatest marvels came in discovering the fragrance of those things that are lovely to God, often hidden in what the world dismisses. The desire to have my mind dwell in this new culture helped me thrive atop this mountain with a heavenly view. It was time for me to rise up in resurrection power.

One day while sitting in my house, I caught a glimpse of movement outside my window. I lifted my gaze to see a shiny silver balloon floating high in the clear blue sky. I'm not sure why, but an impression immediately came to mind that it was for me, a gift from the Lord. So, I ran outside and watched as the wind carried the balloon over the rooftop. Then, in some miraculous shift in the wind current, the balloon began a slow descent, as if it were being carried by angels straight into my hands. When I took hold of it, I couldn't help but marvel at the words inscribed on the balloon: You Are Special! These words were the antithesis of rejection. In an instant, I felt highly valued by the lover of my soul who knew me better than anyone. I could see, hear, and touch His love for me, smell the fragrance of His sweet Spirit, and taste the goodness of my union with Him. The weight in my soul immediately shifted, and I was swept up in His plan of light for my mind, which has continued growing inside me to this day.

Do you believe that God loves you—I mean really believe it? His love is not just for others; it's for you. "The LORD is [your] Shepherd…He makes [you] lie down in green pastures. He leads [you] beside still waters. He restores [your] soul. He leads [you] in paths of righteousness" (Psalm 23:3–4). But wait, there is more. A table is prepared and waiting for you in the presence of your enemies. Yes, He invites you to dine with Him in front of all the rejecting forces of this world (verse 5).

God desires to open the treasure box of Philippians 4:8 and pull out divine truths for you to experience personally. This is your inheritance. Each gift glistens like a precious jewel around your neck or a ring on your finger. Come take your seat next to your King. Let your heart's interest be His kingdom and your place in it. Embrace His thoughts of you. No amount of brokenness, wayward emotion, or despair can separate you from this love, not even your own dark clouds. It is a promise founded in truth, and truth does not change regardless of your feelings.

Trust Him with your future. Instead of taking matters into your own hands, hand them back to Him. He has pulled you out of the grave and is replacing old grave clothes with dazzling linens of light. Let His words to your heart sweep you into His arms as He whispers, "Arise, my love, and come away." Where? Beyond the dark clouds of broken thinking into the blue skies of whatever is true, whatever is just, whatever is honorable, whatever is pure, whatever is lovely, and whatever is worthy of praise.

Made in the USA
Monee, IL
16 April 2021

65970354R10095